Table of Contents

I. DIAGNOSIS

A. Mission

"Gap, Inc. is a brand-builder. We create emotional connections with customers around the world through inspiring product design, unique store experiences, and compelling marketing."

Vision

"Our vision for how we work is built on four pillars:

1. Think: customers first-we consider the needs and value the diversity of thought, experience and perspectives among our customers.
2. Inspire: creativity-we open ourselves to new ideas, tapping into our diversity of perspectives.
3. Do: what right- we treat every customer, supplier and employee with respect.
4. Deliver: results - we strive to create an inclusive environment where employees thrive and generate top performance. Continue

B. Objectives

1. Supply chain

   Our program seeks to ensure that people working at various points along our supply chain the path that our products follow from the concept stage through manufacturing and to our stores – are treated with fairness, dignity and respect.

2. Environment

   Throughout the world, we're finding innovative ways to reduce waste, save energy and water, and incorporate sustainable design into the way we do business.

3. Employees

   Helping the people of Gap Inc. thrive, both personally and professionally, is core to our success as a company. In addition, our Code of Business Conduct sets forth the company's expectation that our employees do what's right and act with integrity in all that they do.

4. Community Investment

   Our vision is simple: to create opportunities for people to own their future and fulfill their personal promise. We aim to change the course of lives for underserved youth in the developed world and women in the developing world by leveraging company assets and the skills, talent, and knowledge of our 134,000 employees to create a deeper impact.

C. Corporate Strategy

A statement by James Glenn K. Murphy, the Chairman of the Board and the Chief Executive Officer at The Gap is given below. The statement has been taken from the company's Annual Report for FY2010.

> "In 2010, Gap Inc. took a big step onto the global retailing stage. With significant advancements in our online and franchise businesses, as well as entry into two more of 4 the world's top 10 retail markets, 2010 will stand out as the year we positioned the company to compete and win globally."

> "We continued to expand share of sales generated from our International and online businesses. In 2006, 14 percent of our sales came from online and International. Now, we are on track to nearly double that percentage within three years."

> "I'm proud we were able to execute on the next phase of our strategy while continuing to deliver attractive financial results for our investors. We achieved double-digit earnings per share growth for the fourth consecutive year, and we're well-positioned to deliver further shareholder value in the years ahead."

> "The hard work of many people across Gap Inc. made these accomplishments possible. For that reason, on the following pages, I've asked a few of our leaders to help answer some questions that have come up in our conversations with shareholders. We have a compelling company strategy, and now it's up to us to execute and deliver for our shareholders, employees and customers."

D. Policies

1 Diversity

As a global company, we know that appreciating and understanding the diversity of our customers, employees and partners around the world helps make us successful. We value the diversity of thought, experience and perspectives of our customers. Embracing diversity stimulates innovation in our products and helps us improve our store experience. That enables us to create an inviting and inclusive place to work and to shop. We maintain our commitment to diversity with workplace policies that ensure we do what's right, and treat our customers – and each other – with integrity and respect.

1. Our Policies

   Our commitment to diversity is reinforced by workplace policies that are essential to how we do business.

2. Equal Opportunity Employer

   We're an equal opportunity employer. All employment decisions are made without regard to race, color, age, gender, gender identity, sexual orientation, religion, marital status, pregnancy, national origin/ancestry, citizenship, physical/mental disabilities, military status or any other basis prohibited by law. Every employee is responsible for preventing discrimination and harassment in the workplace.

3. Zero Means Zero

   At Gap Inc., we work hard to make sure that we treat our customers and each other with integrity and respect, regardless of appearance, skin color, gender, or any other such distinction. We have zero tolerance for discrimination of any kind.

2 Ethical Standards/Code of Conduct

"Our Code of Business Conduct is a commitment we make to our shareholders, customers and each other not only out of a legal obligation, but because it's the right thing to do. Our success is built on trust, along with a reputation for transparency and quality in everything we do. We each make important contributions to protecting our company and its reputation. Recognizing right from wrong, and understanding the ethical implications of our choices, is fundamental to doing what's right at Gap Inc. We are each responsible for applying the standards outlined in our Code of Business Conduct to our work, every day."

3 Suppliers

"While Gap Inc. recognizes that there are different legal and cultural environments in which factories operate throughout the world, Gap Inc's Code of Vendor Conduct sets forth the basic requirements that all factories must meet in order to do business with Gap Inc. This Code is based on internationally accepted labor standards, including the International Labour Organization's core conventions and the Universal Declaration of Human Rights. The Code provides the foundation for Gap Inc.'s ongoing evaluation of a factory's employment practices and environmental compliance."

1. Compliance with Laws

   Factories that produce goods for Gap Inc. shall operate in full compliance with the laws of their respective countries and with all other applicable laws, rules and regulations

2. Environment

   Factories shall comply with all applicable environmental laws and regulations. Where such requirements are less stringent than Gap Inc.'s own, factories are strongly encouraged to meet the standards outlined in Gap Inc.'s statement of environmental principles.

Labor

3. Child Labor

   Factories shall employ only workers who meet the applicable minimum legal age requirement or are at least 15 years of age, whichever is greater. Factories must also comply with all other applicable child labor laws. Factories are encouraged to develop lawful workplace apprenticeship programs for the educational benefit of their workers, provided that all participants meet both Gap Inc.'s minimum age standard of 15 and the minimum legal age requirement.

4. Contract Labor Requirements

   Factories that recruit or employ foreign contract workers shall ensure that these workers are treated fairly and on an equal basis with its local workers.

5. Discrimination

   Factories shall employ workers on the basis of their ability to do the job, not on the basis of their personal characteristics or beliefs.

6. Forced Labor

   Factories shall not use any prison, indentured or forced labor.

7. Freedom of Association and the Right to Collective Bargaining

   Workers are free to join associations of their own choosing. Factories shall not interfere with workers who wish to lawfully and peacefully associate, organize or bargain collectively. The decision whether or not to do so should be made solely by the workers.

8. Humane Treatment

   Factories shall treat all workers with respect and dignity. Factories shall not use corporal punishment or any other form of physical or psychological coercion.

9. Wages & Benefits

Factories shall pay wages and overtime premiums in compliance with all applicable laws. Workers shall be paid at least the minimum legal wages; or a wage that meets local industry standards, whichever is greater. Factories are encouraged to provide wages and benefits that are sufficient to cover workers' basic needs and some discretionary income.

10. Working Hours

Factories shall set working hours in compliance with all applicable laws. While it is understood that overtime is often required in garment production, factories shall carry out operations in ways that limit overtime to a level that ensures humane and productive working conditions.

Working Conditions

11. Occupational Health and Safety

Factories shall comply with all applicable laws and regulations regarding working conditions and shall provide workers with a safe and healthy environment.

12. Dormitory

Factories that provide housing for workers shall keep these facilities clean and safe.

4 Human Resources

"Gap Inc. was founded in 1969 on the principle of doing business responsibly, honestly and ethically. Today, we remain just as committed to working with the highest standards of integrity. Nothing less will do."

Lead and act with integrity

- Understand the Code and periodically review it with your colleagues and teams
- Encourage co-workers and employees to raise questions and concerns
- Ensure employees complete all required compliance training
- Only support the Anti-Retaliation Policy

- Take prompt and effective action where appropriate
- Seek help from Global Integrity and Compliance when needed

E. *Strategic Managers and Board*

1 Senior Level Executives

Name	Job	Title	Board Compensation
Bob L. Martin *Board*: Non Executive Board *Job Title*: Lead Director Since: 2003 Age: 62 Mr. Martin has been the Lead Director at The Gap since 2003. He has served as an Independent Consultant from 1999 to 2002. Mr. Martin served as the President and Chief Executive Officer at Wal-Mart International, a division of Wal-Mart Stores, from 1984 to 1999. Previously, he was a Director at Conn's and SolarWinds. Mr. Martin served as a Director at Dillards from 2003 to 2004, at Edgewater Technology from 1999 to 2005, at Furniture Brands	Chairman of the Board and Chief Executive Board	Executive Officer	$5,945,910 USD

International from 2003 to 2010, at Guitar Center from 2004 to 2007, and at Sabre Holdings Corporation from 1997 to 2007. Currently, he serves as the Chief Executive Officer (part-time) at Mcon Management Services, a consulting company.			
Adrian D. P. Bellamy *Board*: Non Executive Board *Job Title*: Director Since: 1995 Age: 69 Mr. Bellamy has been a Director at The Gap since 1995. He is also the Chairman of the Board at Williams-Sonoma and Reckitt Benckiser. He was the Executive Chairman at the Body Shop International, a personal care retailer, from 2006 to 2008.	Lead Director	Non-Executive Board	
Domenico De Sole *Board*: Non Executive Board	Director	Non-Executive Board	$266,289 USD

Job Title: Director Since: 2004 Age: 67 Mr. De Sole has been a Director at The Gap since 2004. From 1995 to 2004, he served as the President and the Chief Executive Officer at Gucci Group. Currently, Mr. De Sole also serves as a Director at Newell Rubbermaid and is the Chairman at Tom Ford International.			
Robert J. Fisher *Board*: Non Executive Board *Job Title*: Director Since: 1990 Age: 56 Mr. Fisher has been a Director at The Gap since 1990. Previously, he served as the Interim President and Chief Executive Officer at Gap in 2007 and as the Chairman from 2004 to 2007. From 1992 to 1999, Mr. Fisher was an Executive at Gap.	Director	Non-Executive Board	$266,289 USD

From 1995 to 2006, he served as a Director at Sun Microsystems.			
William S. Fisher *Board*: Non Executive Board *Job Title*: Director Since: 2009 Age: 54 Mr. Fisher has been a Director at The Gap since 2009. He is a founder and has been the Chief Executive Officer at Manzanita Capital, a private equity fund, since 2001. Mr. Fisher has held various positions at Gap from 1986 to 1998.	Director	Non-Executive Board	$217,492 USD
Jorge P. Montoya *Board*: Non Executive Board *Job Title*: Director Since: 2004 Age: 64	Director	Non-Executive Board	$209,992 USD

Mr. Montoya has been a Director at The Gap since 2004. He served as the President, Global Snacks & Beverages, and President, Latin America, at The Procter & Gamble Company from 1999 to 2004. From 1996 to 2007, Mr. Montoya served as a Director at Rohm & Hass Company. Currently, he is also a Director at The Kroger.			
Mayo A. Shattuck III *Board*: Non Executive Board *Job Title*: Director Since: 2002 Age: 56 Mr. Shattuck has been a Director at The Gap since 2002. Currently, he also serves as the Chairman, the President and the Chief Executive Officer at Constellation Energy Group and a Director at Capital One Financial Corporation.	Director	Non-Executive Board	$162,042 USD

Katherine Tsang *Board*: Non Executive Board *Job Title*: Director Since: 2010 Age: 53 Ms. Tsang has been a Director at The Gap since 2010. She also serves as the Chairperson at Greater China Standard Chartered Bank. Ms. Tsang has also been the Chairperson at Standard Chartered Bank (Taiwan) since 2009 and the Chairperson at Standard Chartered Bank (Hong Kong) since January 2011. She is also a Director at Baoshan Iron & Steel.	Director	Non-Executive Board	$219,992 USD
Kneeland C.Youngblood *Board*: Non Executive Board *Job Title*: Director Since: 2006 Age: 55	Director	Non-Executive Board	$246,492 USD

Mr.Youngblood has been a Director at The Gap since 2006. He is co-founder and managing partner of Pharos Capital Group. Currently, From 2004 to 2010, Mr.Youngblood served as a Director at Burger King. Currently, he is the Chairman of the Board at American Beacon Funds and a Director at Starwood Hotels and Resorts Worldwide.			
Michelle Banks Board: Senior Management *Job Title*: Executive Vice President, General Counsel, Corporate Secretary and Chief Compliance Officer Since: 2011 Age: 47 Ms. Banks has been Executive Vice President, General Counsel, Corporate Secretary and Chief Compliance Officer at The Gap since 2011. Prior to becoming General Counsel in 2006, she	Director	Non-Executive Board	$163,997 USD

established and led the company's corporate compliance and corporate governance functions. Ms. Banks joined Gap's legal department in 1999. Before joining the company, she served as an in-house Legal Counsel at the NBA's Golden State Warriors, and prior to that, worked in Japan as an American Counsel at ITOCHU Corporation. Ms. Banks was previously associated with several law firms, including Morrison & Foerster in California and New York.			
Jack Calhoun *Board*: Senior Management *Job Title*: President, Banana Republic Mr. Calhoun currently serves as the President, Banana Republic, and a division of The Gap. Before assuming his current role, Mr. Calhoun served as the Executive Vice President, Merchandising and Marketing at Banana Republic. He joined the company in 2003 and prior to that, was the Executive Vice	Executive Vice President, General Senior Management Counsel, Corporate Secretary and Chief Compliance Officer	Senior Management	

President, Brand Management and Advertising at Charles Schwab & Co. Before that, he spent six years leading teams at Foote, Cone & Belding, Citron Haligman Bedecarre, and Young & Rubicam, where he served as General Manager at the San Francisco office. Mr. Calhoun also held marketing positions at Levi Strauss & Company and The Procter & Gamble Company.			
John Ermatinger *Board*: Senior Management *Job Title*: President, Asia Pacific Region Mr. Ermatinger currently serves as the President, Asia Pacific Region at The Gap. Prior to joining the company in 2006, he served at Nike International as the General Manager of Asia Pacific Apparel, overseeing product design, development and sales for sixteen countries, including Japan. Prior to Nike International, Mr. Ermatinger spent 26 years at Levi's serving in various leadership	President, Banana Republic	Senior Management	

positions.			
John T. Keiser *Board*: Senior Management *Job Title*: Executive Vice President and Chief Information Officer Since: 2010 Age: 45 Mr. Keiser has been an Executive Vice President and the Chief Information Officer at The Gap since 2010. Previously, he served as an Executive Vice President and the Chief Information Officer at Limited Brands from 2006 to 2009. Mr. Keiser also served for 12 years at Ernst & Young. He began his career at BellSouth as a Programmer Analyst.	President, Asia Pacific Region	Senior Management	
Toby Lenk *Board*: Senior Management *Job Title*: President, Gap Inc. Direct	Executive Vice President and Chief Senior Management Information	Senior Management	

	Officer		
Mr. Lenk currently serves as the President, Gap Inc. Direct, the e-commerce division of The Gap. Prior to joining the company in 2003, he served as the Chief Executive Officer at GameFly, a leading online video game subscription service he co-founded in 2002. Previously, Mr. Lenk served as the Chief Executive Officer at eToys, an e-commerce business he founded in 1997. Before founding eToys, he served as the Vice President, Corporate Strategic Planning at The Walt Disney Company. Currently, Mr. Lenk serves as a Director at GameFly.			
Arthur Peck *Board*: Senior Management *Job Title*: President, Gap North America Since: 2011 Age: 55 Mr. Peck has been the President, Gap North America at The Gap since	President, Gap Inc. Direct	Senior Management	

2011. Prior to that, he served as the Acting President, Gap Inc. Outlet from February 2008 to October 2008. Mr. Peck was the President, Gap Inc. Outlet from 2008 to 2011 and the Executive Vice President, Strategy and Operations at Gap from 2005 to 2011. Before joining Gap in 2005, he served as a Senior Vice President and Director at The Boston Consulting Group from 1982 to 2005. Currently, Mr. Peck serves as a trustee on the Board at Gap Foundation.			
Stanley P. Raggio *Board*: Senior Management *Job Title*: Executive Vice President, Global Supply Chain Since: 2010 Age: 54 Mr. Raggio has been the Executive Vice President, Global Supply Chain at The Gap since 2010. He joined the company in 1990, and served as the Vice President, International	President, Gap North America	Senior Management	$3,727,611 USD

Logistics from 1990¬¬ to 1995, ¬¬and as the Senior Vice President, International Sourcing and Logistics from 1995 to 2002. He retired from Gap in 2002. Mr. Raggio rejoined the company in 2006 and served as Senior Vice President, Gap International Sourcing from 2006 to 2010.			
Eva Sage-Gavin *Board*: Senior Management *Job Title*: Executive Vice President, Global Human Resources and Corporate Affairs Since: 2010 Age: 52 Ms. Sage-Gavin has been the Executive Vice President, Global Human Resources and Corporate Affairs at The Gap since 2010. She joined the company in 2003. Previously, Ms. Sage-Gavin served at Sun Microsystems as the Senior Vice President, Human Resources.	Executive Vice President, Global Senior Management Supply Chain	Senior Management	

She also served as the Senior Vice President, Human Resources at The Walt Disney Company. Ms. Sage-Gavin also served in various senior human resources leadership positions at The PepsiCo Corporation, including its Taco Bell division, and at Xerox Corporation.			
Sabrina Simmons *Board*: Senior Management *Job Title*: Executive Vice President and Chief Financial Officer Since: 2008 Age: 47 Ms. Simmons has been an Executive Vice President and the Chief Financial Officer at Gap since 2008. She joined the company in 2001. Before joining Gap, Ms. Simmons was the Chief Financial Officer and an Executive Member of the Board of Directors at Sygen International. Prior to that, she spent five years at Levi Strauss where Ms. Simmons served as an Assistant Treasurer. Ms.	Executive Vice President, Global Senior Management Human Resources and Corporate Affairs	Senior Management	

Simmons also spent several years at Hewlett Packard Company and KPMG. She is a California Certified Public Accountant.			
Stephen Sunnucks *Board*: Senior Management *Job Title*: President, Europe and International Strategic Alliances Mr. Sunnucks currently serves as the President, Europe and International Strategic Alliances at The Gap. Prior to joining the company, Mr. Sunnucks spent four years as the Chief Executive Officer at New Look. He also held senior leadership roles at Marks & Spencer, Sainsbury, and the Burton Group (now Arcadia) in his 30 year career.	Executive Vice President and Chief Senior Management Financial Officer	Senior Management	$3,287,133 USD
J. Tom Wyatt *Board*: Senior Management *Job Title*: President, Old Navy Since: 2008	President, Europe and International Senior Management Strategic Alliances	Senior Management	

Age: 55 Mr. Wyatt has been the President, Old Navy at The Gap since 2008. He joined the company as the President of Gap Body in 2006. Later, in 2007, Mr. Wyatt was appointed the Head of the Gap Inc. Outlet. Prior to joining the company, he served as the President and Chief Executive Officer at Cutter & Buck. Mr. Wyatt also served as the President at Warnaco Intimate Apparel, a global designer and manufacturer. He spent more than 20 years at Vanity Fair Corporation, serving as President of Vanity Fair Intimates and Vanity Fair Intimates Coalition.			
David Zoba *Board*: Senior Management *Job Title*: Senior Vice President, Global Real Estate Mr. Zoba currently serves as the Senior Vice President, Global Real Estate at The Gap. Previously, he served as the Principal and Chief Operating Officer at Steiner + Associates. Before that, Mr. Zoba	President, Old Navy	Senior Management	

served at Galyan's Trading Company and The Limited. He started his career as a real estate attorney on Wall Street.			
	Senior Vice President, Global Real Senior Management Estate	Senior Management	$3,866,700 USD

2 Corporate Governance

1. Responsibilities

General Responsibilities

- Submit the minutes of all committee meetings and regularly report to the board of directors on committee matters.
- Review and reassess the adequacy of this Charter annually and propose to the board any changes to the charter.
- Review and discuss with management a Compensation Discussion and Analysis and prepare a report of the committee on executive compensation in accordance with SEC requirements to be included in the company's annual proxy statement.
- Annually assess the committee's performance.
- Perform such other functions assigned by law, the company's charter or bylaws, or the board.

Compensation Responsibilities

- Review and approve the company's compensation philosophy.

- Review and approve on an annual basis the corporate goals and objectives with respect to compensation for the CEO. The committee will evaluate at least once a year the CEO's performance in light of these established goals and objectives and based upon these evaluations shall determine and approve the CEO's annual compensation, including salary, bonus, incentive and equity compensation.

- Review and approve on an annual basis the compensation structure for the company's other officers, including specific approval of salary, bonus, incentive and equity compensation for executive officers.

- Review the company's executive incentive compensation and other equity-based plans and recommend changes in such plans to the board as needed. The committee may exercise the authority of the board with respect to the administration of such plans.

- Periodically review and make recommendations to the board regarding the compensation of non-management directors, including board and committee retainers, meeting fees, equity-based compensation, and such other forms of compensation as the committee may consider appropriate.

- Review and approve for executive officers, including the CEO, any employment, severance or change in control agreements.

- Approve any loans to employees at the Vice President level or above as allowed by law.

Responsibilities Related to Management Development

- Review development and retention initiatives for senior management positions, including the CEO.

- Review and approve the succession plan for the CEO.

- Ensure succession plans are in place for senior management positions reporting to the CEO.

- Maintain visibility to the appointment and removal of executive officers.

2. Board Committees

Existing Committees

- Audit and Finance, composed solely of Independent directors. The Audit and Finance Committee assists the board in fulfilling its oversight responsibilities relating to the integrity of the financial statements, compliance with legal and regulatory requirements, the independent accountant's qualifications and independence, the performance of the internal audit function and the performance of the independent accountant, and to handle such other matters as formalized in the Audit and Finance Committee Charter.

- Compensation and Management Development, composed solely of Independent directors who also meet the requirements of Section 16 of the Securities Exchange Act of 1934 and Section 162(m) of the Internal Revenue Code. The functions of the Compensation and Management Development Committee are to evaluate and determine compensation policies, including level and form, for all corporate and divisional officers and certain employees, to recommend compensation for Non-Management directors, to advise senior management on policy and strategy regarding succession planning and the development and retention of senior executives and management teams, and to handle such other matters as formalized in the Compensation and Management Development Committee Charter.

- Governance and Nominating, composed solely of Independent directors. As set forth under the company's Bylaws, the board has the discretion to form new committees or dissolve existing committees depending upon the circumstances. The Governance and Nominating Committee makes recommendations to the board on all matters concerning corporate governance and directorship practices as formalized in the Governance and Nominating Committee Charter, including development of corporate governance guidelines, evaluation of the board, committees and individual directors, and identification and selection of new board nominees.

Our Board of Directors currently has 11 members and has determined that 10 are independent under NYSE rules. We require 100 percent membership independence on our three committees:

Director	Audit & Finance	Compensation & Mgmt Devel.	Gov'nce & Nominating
Independent			
Adrian D. P. Bellamy		C	M
Domenico De Sole		M	
Robert J. Fisher			M
William S. Fisher			
Bella Goren	M		
Bob L. Martin		M	C
Jorge P. Montoya	M		
Mayo A. Shattuck III	C		M
Katherine Tsang		M	
Other			
Glenn K. Murphy			

3. **Director Compensation**

   1. Board Compensation Review.

      The Compensation and Management Development Committee periodically reviews and makes recommendations to the board concerning the level and form of compensation of the Non-Management directors.

The committee's recommendation, which is discussed and evaluated by the full board, is based on both an assessment of the best practices of other companies and the particular circumstances of this board. Changes in board compensation, if any, must be approved by the full board.

2. Director Compensation

The Non-Management directors' annual base retainer is currently $70,000 per annum, plus an attendance fee of $1,500 for each regularly scheduled committee meeting attended. Non-management directors who primarily reside outside of North America receive a fee of $2,000 for attendance at each board and/or committee meeting requiring travel to the United States. The Governance and Nominating Committee Chair receives an additional retainer of $10,000 per annum. The Audit and Finance Committee Chair and the Compensation and Management Development Committee Chair each receive an additional retainer of $20,000 per annum. The Lead Independent director receives an additional retainer of $20,000 per annum. In addition, Non-Management directors are eligible to receive stock unit awards according to a pre-determined formula as follows:

- Upon appointment each new Non-Management director is awarded units equal to $125,000 at the then-current fair market value

- Annually, each continuing Non-Management director is awarded units equal to $125,000 at the then-current fair market value (recently appointed Non-Management directors first annual stock unit grant shall be prorated based on the number of days that the director has served between the appointment date and the first annual stock unit grant). Normally, the stock units are immediately vested as of the award date with payment in shares deferred for 3 years unless further deferred at the election of the Non-Management director.

3. Travel.

All Non-Management directors' reasonable travel arrangements related to attending board, committee or company business meetings are made by the company. Alternatively, the company can reimburse the Non-Management director for reasonable travel expenses.

4. Discount.

All directors are eligible to receive discounts on company merchandise consistent with the terms of the Employee Merchandise Discount Policy.

F. Generic Industry Type

1. Hirschman- Herfindahl Index

Hirschman-Herfindahl Index (HHI)	The Herfindahl Hirschman Index (HHI) is a measurement used to understand the level of competition that exists within a market or industry, as well as give an indication of how the distribution of market share occurs across the companies included in the index.

Less than 100	Highly Competitive
Between 100-1,000	Market Not Concentrated
Between 1,000-1,800	Moderately Concentrated
Above 1,800	Highly Concentrated

Using the four major players, the Herfindahl-Hirschman Index for the Family Clothing Stores in the U.S. industry is calculated as follows:

$HHI = (13.2^2) + (13.1^2) + (10.6^2) + (3.8^2) = 472.65$

Global Apparel Retail

Using the four major players, the Herfindahl-Hirschman Index for the Global Apparel Retail industry is calculated as follows:

$HHI = (1.8^2) + (1.2^2) + (1.1^2) + (1.0^2) = 6.9$

When comparing the HHI for the clothing industry, domestically versus globally, it is very obvious that both industries are extremely competitive with many different players. With an HHI of 10,000 being the highest, the small HHI of 472.65 for the U.S. Family Clothing Stores Industry and the even smaller 6.89 HHI for the Global Apparel Retail Industry, it is obvious that the amount of competition in both industries is fierce

2. Industry Economic Characteristics

Industry definition	This industry comprises of establishments primarily engaged in retailing a general line of new clothing for men, women and children, without specializing in sales for an individual gender or age group. These establishments may provide basic alterations such as hemming, taking in or letting out seams and lengthening or shortening sleeves. Retail is a mature industry with a cyclical business cycle. The industry is saturated with competitors, established brands, and has low barriers to entry.

The Gap is one of America's most recognized brands and is famous for its casual wear. The company retails a range of jeans, t-shirts and khakis in more than 3,000 stores in the United States, the United Kingdom, Canada, France, Japan and Ireland. Built on its iconic basics brand, the company has expanded to include urban hip brands like Banana Republic and Old Navy. The Gap brands include Gap, GapKids, BabyGap, GapBody and Gap Outlet. Even as an international company, an overwhelming majority of sales are generated domestically.

Life Cycle Stage	**Mature**	Regulation Level	**Med**
Revenue Volatility	**Low**	Technology Change	
Capital Intensity	**Medium**	Barriers to Entry	**Med**
Industry Assistance	**Low**	Industry Globalization	
Concentration Level	**Medium**	Competition Level	

The primary activities of this industry include:
- Family Clothing Stores
- Unisex Clothing Stores

- Western Wear Stores

The major products and services this industry include:

- Women's formal wear
- Women's casual wear
- Other women's wear
- Men's formal wear
- Men's casual wear
- Other men's wear
- Children's wear

Similar Industries include:

- **44811** Men's Clothing Stores
  - This industry retails a general line of new men's and boys' clothing sleeves.
- **44812** Women's Clothing Stores
  - This industry is primarily engaged in retailing a general line of new women's, misses' and juniors' clothing, including maternity wear.
- **44813** Children's and Infants' Clothing Stores
  - This industry retails a general line of new children's and infants' clothing.

- **45211** Department Store in the US
  - This industry, known as department stores, retails a wide range of the following new products with no one merchandise line predominating: apparel, furniture, appliances and home furnishings; and selected additional items, such as paint, hardware, toiletries, cosmetics, photographic equipment, jewelry, toys, and sporting goods. Merchandise lines are normally

	arranged in separate departments.
	<ul><li>**44819** - Lingerie, Swimwear & Bridal Stores<ul><li>This industry retails specialized new apparel, such as raincoats, bridal gowns, leather coats, fur apparel and swimwear.</li></ul></li><li>**45331**- Used Goods Stores<ul><li>This industry retails secondhand clothing.</li></ul></li><li>**45411a** E-Commerce & Online Auctions in the US<ul><li>This industry provides websites for and facilitating consumer-to –consumer or business-to-business trade in clothing on an auction and sales basis using the internet</li></ul></li><li>**45411b** Mail Order in the US<ul><li>This industry retails clothing via mail catalogs or television, and from catalog showrooms or mail-order houses and provides internet and mail-order sales.</li></ul></li></ul>
Market size and growth rate	Retail spending on clothing in America lost momentum over the five years to 2012. The rapidly growing national unemployment rate, falling per capita disposable income and uncertainty about future finances made numerous consumers cautious with their discretionary expenditures. However, compared with other clothing retail industries, family clothing stores have performed better over the five years to 2012. During this period, IBIS World expects that revenue for the Family Clothing Stores industry will decline at an annualized rate of 0.1% to $91.6 billion in 2012. In comparison, the Men's Clothing Stores industry's revenue is expected to drop at an average annual rate of 2.9% over the same five-year period. The US real GDP increased in 2010 by 3.8% following a 1.7% decrease in 2009. Positive GDP growth is the result of the recession ending and is an indication that the economy is on the rise. An upward change in real GDP is an excellent indication of economic growth which will assist future growth for Gap, Inc.

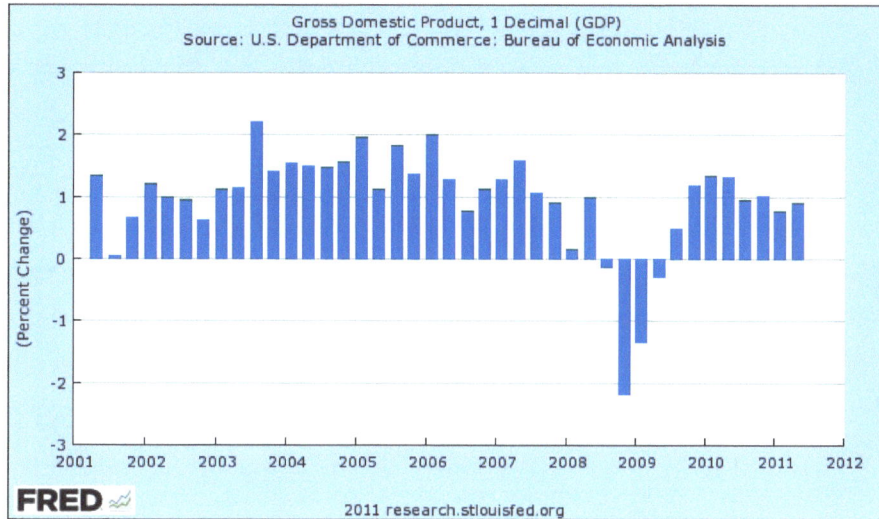

Gross Domestic Product, 1 Decimal (GDP)
Source: U.S. Department of Commerce: Bureau of Economic Analysis

While revenue for the Family Clothing Stores industry is slated to record an average annual decline of 0.1% over the five years to 2012, IBIS World forecasts a relatively strong rebound.

Family Clothing Store

Revenue Outlook

Year	Revenue $ million	Growth %
2013	93,576.6	2.1
2014	96,113.2	2.7
2015	99,007.2	3.0
2016	101,003.7	2.0
2017	102,633.1	1.6
2018	104,204.9	1.5

Revenue is expected to recover 2.1% in 2013 and grow at an average annual rate of 2.3% to $102.6 billion over the five years to 2017. As the economy recovers and consumer sentiment recovers at an estimated average annual rate of 2.8%, consumers will likely buy clothes for fashion rather than just for necessity. New stores will open to meet the growing to an estimated 50,254 in 2017.

With personal disposable income growing at an annual rate of 1.6%, consumers will be less price-sensitive and more responsive to advertising and branding. The level of consumer confidence affects general household expenditure. Consumer sentiment is an important indicator for future shopping preferences. When consumer perceptions of the economy are positive and confidence is high, households tend to spend more freely on items such as clothing. This driver is expected to increase during 2012, creating a potential opportunity for the industry.

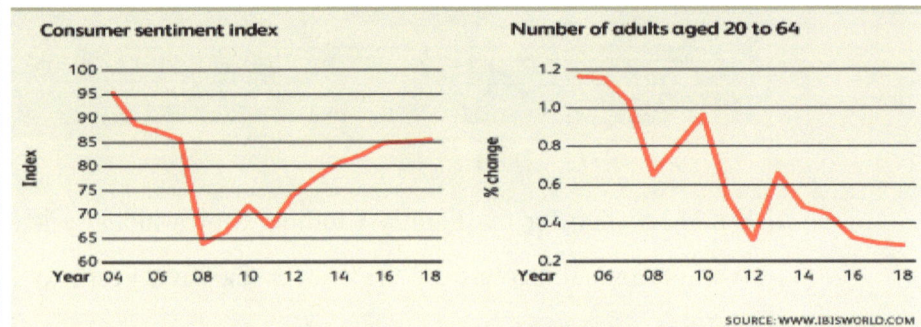

According to IBIS World, the preference for high-quality and prominent brands will overshadow the need to save money, especially as the brand-conscious Generation Y begins to account for a more significant portion of the industry's primary market.

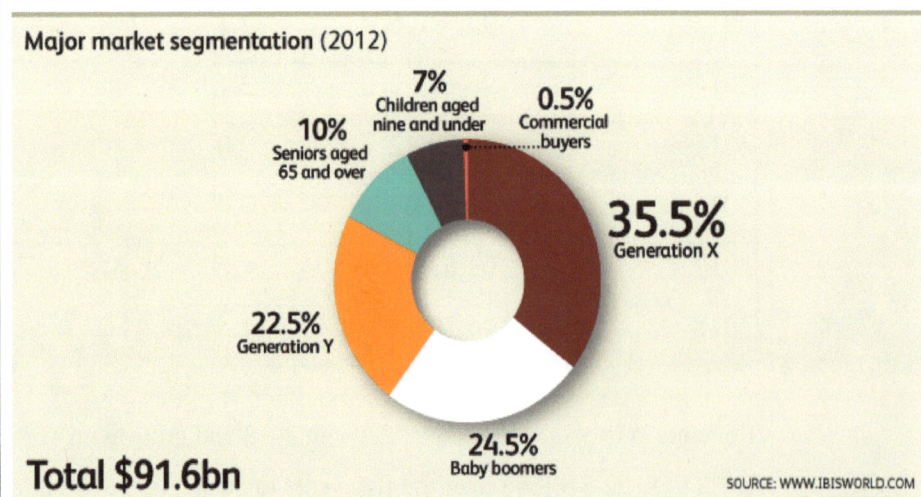

Major market segmentation (2012)

Total $91.6bn

SOURCE: WWW.IBISWORLD.COM

Currently, Generation X contains the largest market segment for the Family Clothing Stores industry bringing in 35.5% of revenue. It has grown slightly over the five

	years to 2012 as more of these consumers have children. Generation Y makes up only 22.5% of the industry's market. These consumers are more brand-conscious and prefer to shop at specialty retailers that carry more visible brands.
	Overall, there has been a modest growth in recent years. In 2010, total revenue was $1,439.7 billion representing a compound annual growth rate of 2.7% within a four year span.
Key rivals & market share	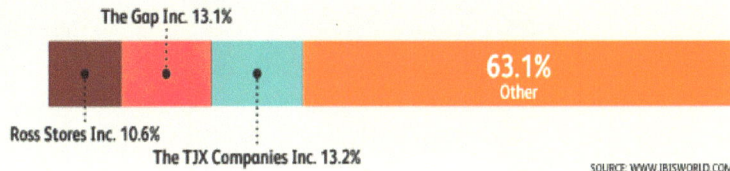 **Major players** (Market share) The Gap Inc. 13.1% 63.1% Other Ross Stores Inc. 10.6% The TJX Companies Inc. 13.2% SOURCE: WWW.IBISWORLD.COM A major player is a company that generates more than 5% of the industries revenue. The chart shows the market share of each major player and the collective concentration of all dominant industry players. In 2012, the top four industry participants (TJX Companies, The Gap, Ross Stores and Abercrombie & Fitch) will collectively account for 40.7% of total industry revenue. Over the five years to 2012, concentration has increased. Two of the top four operators, TJX and Ross Stores, target price-conscious consumers with their low in-store prices, allowing them to grow strongly during the recession. Gap carries products in all price ranges and backs its product with the trusted Gap brand.

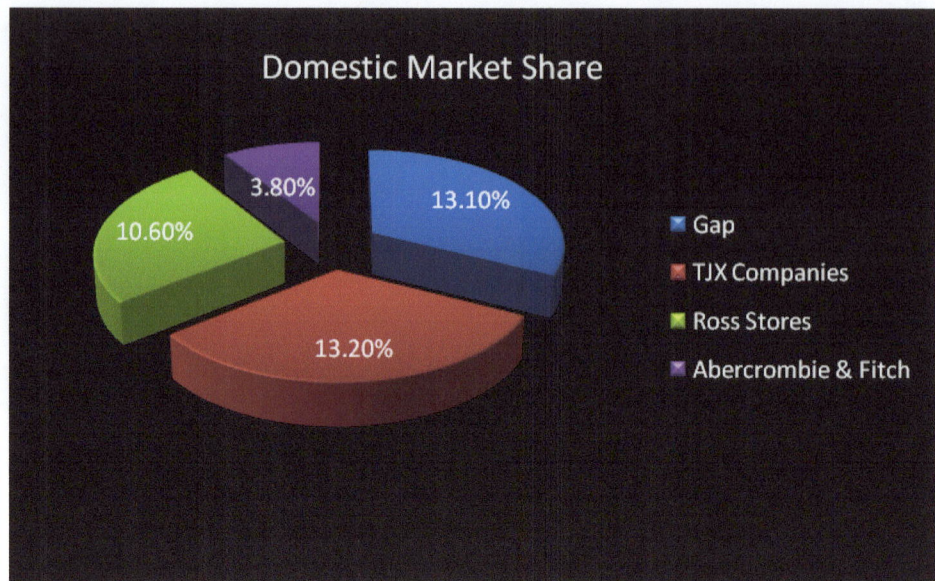

The increased market share concentration can be attributed to these retailers' positions within the industry. Affordable prices and recognizable brands have helped them through the economic recession. IBIS World forecasts that concentration will remain relatively steady over the five years to 2017 as consumers regain their purchasing power and switch from off-price retailers like TJX and Ross to higher-priced, higher-quality brands like the Gap's Banana Republic segment.

The United States accounts for 29.6% of the global apparel retail industry value. Europe accounts for a further 37.3% of the global industry.

Table 3: United States apparel retail industry segmentation II: % share, by value, 2009(e)	
Category	% Share
Europe	37.3%
United States	29.6%
Asia-Pacific	25.5%
Rest of the World	7.7%
Total	100%
Source: Datamonitor	DATAMONITOR

Figure 3:   United States apparel retail industry segmentation II: % share, by value, 2009(e)

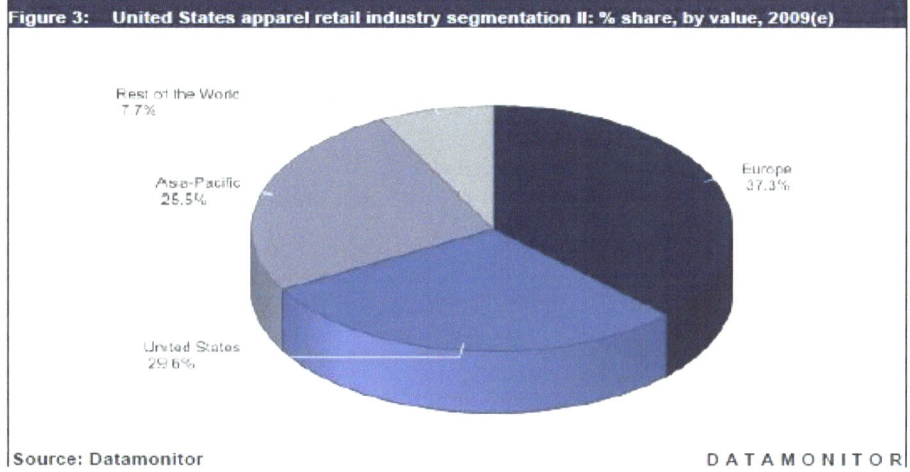

Source: Datamonitor   DATAMONITOR

Wal-mart is the leading player in the global apparel, accessories and luxury good market, generating a 1.8 share of the markets value and H&M accounts for a further 1.2 of the market.

Scope of competitive rivalry	The Gap, Inc.'s large product line and distribution exposes Gap to intense competition. Gap competes with local and national department stores, specialty and discount store chains, independent retail stores, and online businesses that market similar lines of merchandise. To be successful, brand recognition is vital.
	Family clothing stores typically compete with similar stores that are located within their prime market area. Consumers will favor stores that are located closer to home and only shop further away when seeking a specific item or brand. Family clothing retailers' major external competitors are men's clothing stores, women's clothing stores, children's and Infants' clothing stores and department stores. Stores specializing in particular market segments offer these consumers a wider variety to choose from and well-known brands that cater to current trends. Department stores compete with family clothing retailers on selection and price. They can give consumers discounts or stock a larger variety of brand names to reel them in. Internet-based retailers also compete against family clothing stores. Their shop-from-home format allows consumers the convenience and ease not found in traditional brick and mortar shops. During the recession, discount stores were more attractive alternatives to money-conscious consumers.
	Price remains a major basis of competition for operators, particularly those that target low-to-middle-income earners. Retailers like TJX and Ross Stores target value-conscious consumers and offer discounts off department store prices. During the recession, these stores grew despite the low consumer sentiment and disposable income levels.
	Clothing retailers are affected by competition from substitutes such as department stores and specialty men's and women's clothing stores. When consumers buy more clothing from alternative stores, demand for clothing from industry establishments will likely decrease. This driver is expected to increase slowly during 2012, posing a potential threat to the industry.

	Traditional competitors of the Family Clothing Stores industry are retailers like department stores and specialty women's and men's clothing stores. However, during the Great Recession, even the competition did not fare well. Department stores are expected to lose revenue at an average annual rate of 3.1% over the five years to 2012, while women's and men's clothing retailers have recorded average annual revenue drops of 0.9% and 4.2%, respectively best deals on their purchases. The industry also faces the looming threat of competition from the quickly expanding E-Commerce and Online Auctions industry, which is forecast to grow at an average annual rate of 8.8% to $334.3 billion over the five years to 2017. Instead of physically walking around a store in search of a clothing item, consumers are likely to more fully embrace online shopping. The industry is forecast to grow steadily over the five years to 2017, leading to saturation and limited expansion opportunities. For players to succeed, they must differentiate themselves from the competition, both within and outside the Family Clothing Stores industry. Retailers will likely move into less visible markets and focus on niche products like plus-sized clothing or fashion-forward apparel to continue growing. Designs that showcase a unique style will likely be accepted quickly by the growing Generation Y market, whose members are brand and image sensitive. There is room for large numbers of smaller players. Major increases in capacity may be costly to smaller players if they require the outlay of opening additional outlets, less so if they can be accomplished by taking on more staff on a flexible basis. Future market performance encourages market entry which will intensify rivalry within the market. Overall, rivalry is assessed to be moderate.
Concentration vs. fragmentation	This is a fairly fragmented industry. As is the case with many retailing industries, the Family Clothing Stores industry geographic spread follows that of population. The Southeast region accounts for about 25.2% of population and 28.5% of total family clothing stores. Within the region, Florida has the highest concentration of industry locations, accounting for 8.3% of the total. The state also holds 6.0% of the country's

population. The higher occurrence of establishments than inhabitants signifies that the average Floridian spends more on family clothes than the average American. The West is estimated to account for 17.8% of industry establishments and 17.0% of the nation's population. In this region, California accounts for the highest number of family clothing stores and population, with 12.6% and 12.1%, respectively. In fact, California is the most populous state and, fittingly, its portion of industry establishments is the largest of any state. The fairly equal portions of establishment numbers and population mean that Californians typically spend an average amount on family clothing. In the Mid-Atlantic region, consumers spend less on the industry's product than the average American. The portion of population (15.7%) outweighs the portion of store locations (15.0%). In this area, New York is the most densely-populated state, with the most people and the most stores: 6.4% of the nation's total and 6.1% of industry establishments, respectively.

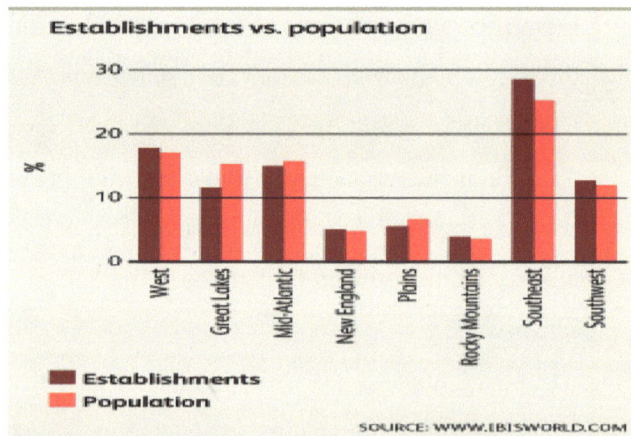

Family clothing stores are generally clustered near or in metropolitan areas. For this reason, California, Florida and Texas have the highest concentration of industry establishments. Each state has multiple big cities which are target markets for the industry's participants. However, as retail increasingly moves online, the relation of distribution locations to population becomes less important. For example, internet retailer Amazon.com has fulfillment facilities in less populous states, including Kentucky, Nevada and Indiana. In light of this trend, IBIS World expects a shift in establishments to follow low operational costs.

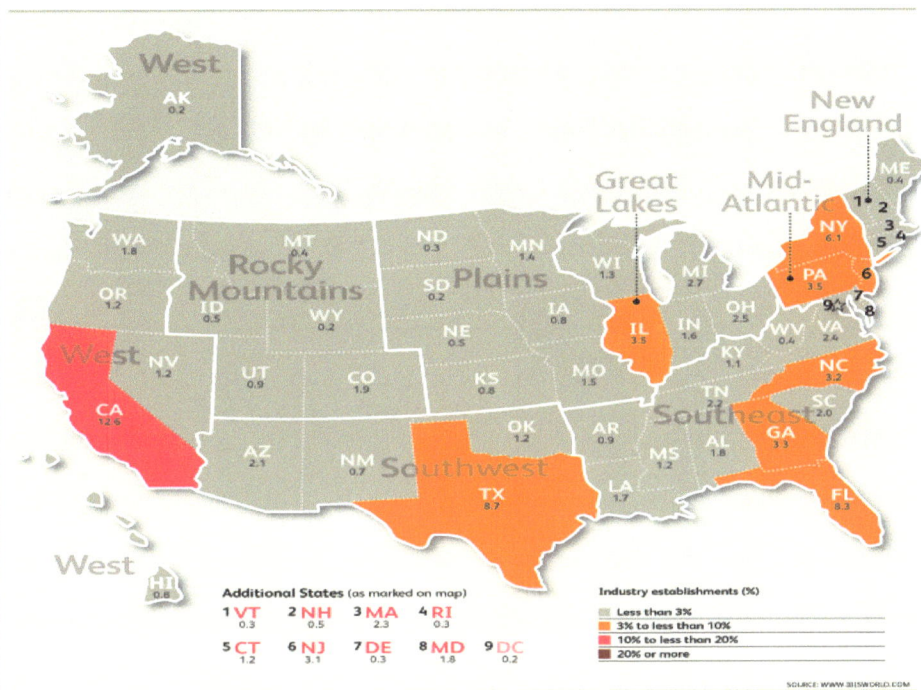

The Global market is fragmented. The company has significantly expanded the international reach of its brands through its franchise stores, online presence and company-operated stores. In 2006, Gap Inc. operated in eight countries and only sold products online in the United States. Today, products are available through stores in more than 40 countries and available online to customers in about 90 countries worldwide.

For major markets, the company typically enters with brand-building flagship stores, followed by outlet and smaller stores in outlying areas and an online expression of the brand. This model can be applied to Gap and Banana Republic, and over time, Old Navy. For other markets, the franchise model allows the company to expand successfully. Gap Inc. is strongly positioned to continue to grow its share of the $1.4 trillion global apparel market through its global growth strategy.

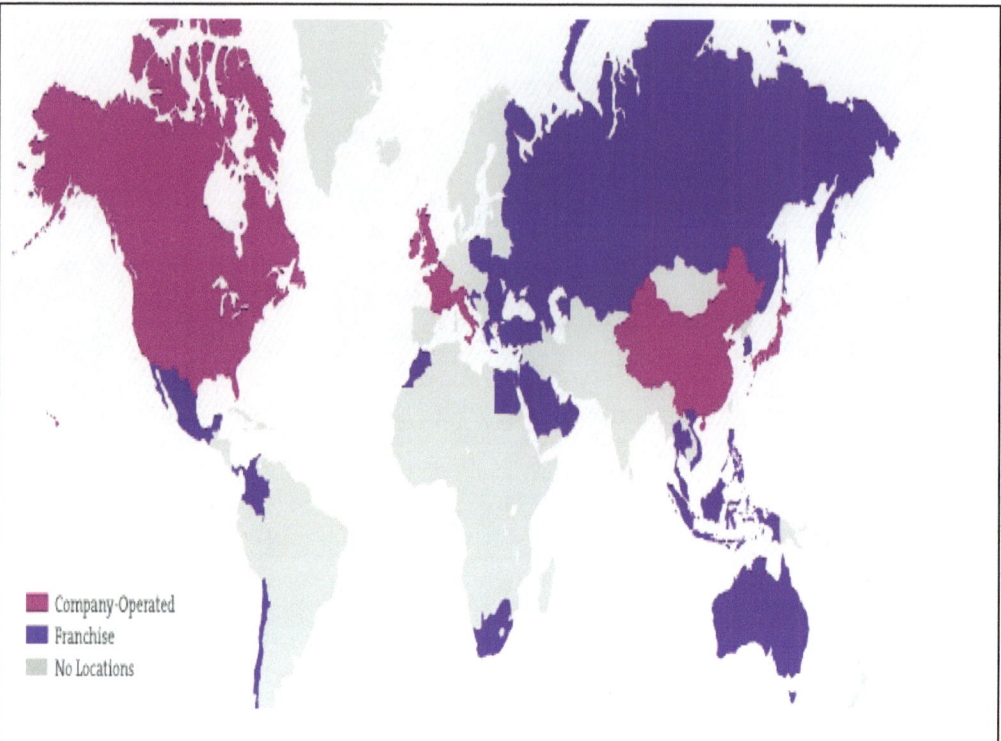

Company-Operated
Franchise
No Locations

The illustration below provides the numerical figure for company stores and franchise store in countries that Gap, Inc. operates within.

As of 10/27/2012	Gap			
	Stores		Online (countries)	
	Company Stores	Franchise Stores	Served by company website	Served by 3rd party
USA*	918		✔	
Canada	98		✔	✔
Mexico		35		✔
Panama		2		✔
Other Countries				✔
North America	**1,016**	**37**	**2**	**13**
United Kingdom	146		✔	
France	37		✔	
Ireland	3		✔	
Italy	10		✔	
Belgium			✔	
Bulgaria		1		
Croatia		1		
Greece		7		
Netherlands			✔	
Poland		2		
Romania		1		
Russia		14		
Serbia		1		
Ukraine		3		
Other Countries			✔	✔

North America	**1,016**	**37**	**2**	**13**
United Kingdom	146		✔	
France	37		✔	
Ireland	3		✔	
Italy	10		✔	
Belgium			✔	
Bulgaria		1		
Croatia		1		
Greece		7		
Netherlands			✔	
Poland		2		
Romania		1		
Russia		14		
Serbia		1		
Ukraine		3		
Other Countries			✔	✔
Europe	**196**	**30**	**22**	**2**
Japan	144		✔	
China	31			✔
Armenia		1		
Bahrain		1		✔
Cyprus		1		
Georgia		1		
Indonesia		6		✔
Israel		6		
Jordan		3		✔
Kazakhstan		3		
Kuwait		2		✔
Lebanon		1		
Malaysia		8		
Oman		1		✔

Country	Col1	Col2	Col3	Col4
Philippines		8		✔
Qatar		2		✔
Saudi Arabia		23		✔
Singapore		5		✔
South Korea		26		
Thailand		7		✔
Turkey		33		
U.A.E.		10		✔
Vietnam		4		
Other Countries				✔
Asia	**175**	**152**	**1**	**21**
Australia		3		✔
Guam**		2		
New Zealand				✔
Oceania	**0**	**5**	**0**	**2**
Chile		3		✔
Colombia		1		✔
Other Countries				✔
South America	**0**	**4**	**0**	**8**
Egypt		3		✔
Morocco		1		
South Africa		4		✔
Other Countries				
Africa	**0**	**8**	**0**	**2**

Number of Buyers	The number of buyers comprise of individuals who view clothing as a necessity. The retail industry consumers include men, women and children who purchase clothing. According IBIS World, the household consist of about 99.5% of the market for this product. Practically all buyers are individual consumers and this fact weakens buyer negotiation power. Additionally, consumers view clothing as an abstract concept which allows one to express their individualism which weakens buyer power for the reason that clothing style is individualized. According to Data Monitor, there are other possible sources of apparel, such as home-made clothing; generally the demographic and psychological significance of retail garments is highly important to consumers, further weakening buyer power. There has been a prominent increasingly demand for stores providing low cost consumer apparel. Discount apparel retail is targeted to consumers within the price sensitivity segment. In order to succeed, a company must compete intensely on price, selling clothes as cheaply as possible from their own suppliers Women's wear is the largest segment of the apparel retail industry in the

	United States, accounting for 53% of the industry's total value. The menswear segment accounts for a further 31.4% of the industry **Table 2:** United States apparel retail industry segmentation I:% share, by value, 2009(e) | Category	% Share
Womenswear	53.0%
Menswear	31.4%
Childrenswear	15.6%
Total	100% | Source: Datamonitor D A T A M O N I T O R **Figure 2:** United States apparel retail industry segmentation I:% share, by value, 2009(e) Childrenswear 15.6% Womenswear 53.0% Menswear 31.4% Source: Datamonitor D A T A M O N I T O R
Demand Determinant	The demand for family clothing is affected by a number of varying factors. As noted earlier, clothing is a necessity and price is a vital determinant of demand. When the recession occurred, consumer confidence and personal disposable income levels were at a low and many Americans were shopping with a budget. In other words, consumers were looking for a bargain and promotions or sales offered by family clothing stores had an effect on demand. According to IBIS World, consumers' purchasing patterns are influenced by the strength and power of brand names. Brand perception may help retailers generate higher sales over their competitors and the largest operators are also the most recognizable: The Gap, TJX and Ross Stores. Keep in mind, each one of these stores bring to the table a specific and unique style of clothing to consumers.
Degree of product differentiation	Retailers can differentiate themselves through the styles of clothing that they offer. It is vital for apparel retail industry to understand that consumers view clothing as an abstract concept which allows one to express their individualism. The importance of style and fashion is today's society is extremely important and offering diversified products and a variety of options allows the consumers to keep up with the changing and unpredictable trends. Classifications of trends include: fashionable, demographic,

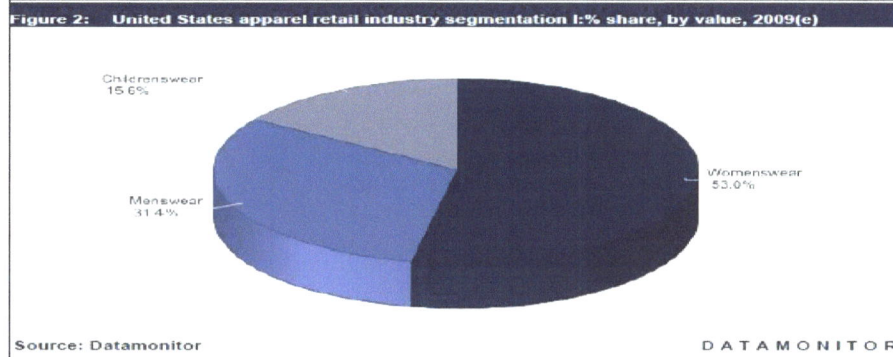

	offering, social responsibility and etc. For example, health and wellness is classified as a demographic trend, which is a driver behind Gap Inc's athletic apparel. In the year of 2006, Gap launched a campaign for (PRODUCT) RED, a for-benefit brand designed to help eliminate AIDS in Africa. Corporate social responsibility adds value to products and consumers wanted to partake in contributing a sense of hope and making a difference in the lives of others. "Within one year, (PRODUCT) RED has contributed more than $45 million to the Global Fund to finance programs that help women and children affected by HIV/AIDS in Africa," said Marka Hansen, president of Gap Brand North America. It is also important to offer a wide wider variety of items to suit different occasions. During the past five years, the women's casual wear product segment has declined from about 36.0% to 32.6%. The demand for men's clothing is much more fickle than demand for women's clothing. During the recession, IBIS World estimates that this segment has declined from representing 37.0% of revenue in 2007 to its current 33.4%. Children's apparel accounts for a much smaller 7.5% of revenue. This is because the average price of kids' clothes is significantly lower than the price for a formal suit jacket or a designer dress. **Products and services segmentation (2012)** 7.2% Other men's wear 7.5% Children's wear 8.8% Men's formal wear 13.1% Other women's wear 32.6% Women's casual wear 13.4% Women's formal wear 17.4% Men's casual wear **Total $91.6bn** SOURCE: WWW.IBISWORLD.COM As stated earlier, consumers in this market are often sensitive to price changes, but style, product range and comfort are also important factors. Retailers such as Gap, Inc. need to target particular product segments, such as casual wear or plus-sizes, in order to differentiate themselves from their intra-industry competitors.
Product innovation	Diversity is the rich variety reflected in Gap, Inc.'s work environment and marketplace. Embracing diversity creates an atmosphere that encourages

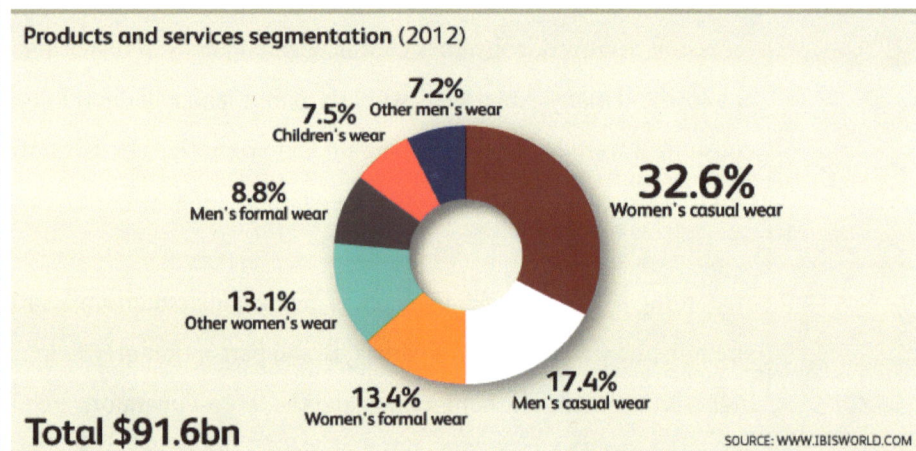

	product innovation all the diversity within Gap, Inc.'s employee population enables the company to generate the innovation and creativity necessary to better serve customers. Each brand is also pursuing new product categories and product partnerships. For example, Old Navy has launched licensing, jewelry and introduced new product at its register lanes, while Gap announced a partnership with Diane von Furstenberg for a line of kids' product. Gap also had a successful (PRODUCT) RED collection for men and women comprised of items rooted in classic Gap product categories such as T-shirts, hoodies, jeans and accessories. Due to its success, they plan on introducing babyGap and GapKids introduced (PRODUCT) RED collections made especially for babies and kids including bodysuits for babies with playful "(RED)" words like DELIVE(RED) and DIAPE(RED), and T-shirts with kid-inspired graphics and embellishments. All of these items are branded Gap (PRODUCT) RED and feature subtle, distinct details inspired by (RED). Gap Inc continues to expand its global online expansion and extend exceptional online experience worldwide. The e-commerce sites will feature Gap Inc.'s innovative "Universality" platform, which brings the Gap and Banana Republic brands together on one, easy to navigate e-commerce platform. Customers can seamlessly shop Gap, GapKids, babyGap and Banana Republic with one shopping basket and one checkout. Since the site is open 24 hours a day, seven days a week, customers can shop whenever it is most convenient for them.
Key success factors	**Important Key Success Factors include:** - **Having a clear market position:** A clear market position projects a clear and consistent company image. - **Ability to control stock on hand:** Adequate stock control is vital in

	order to reduce inventory costs and increase stock turns. • **Production of goods currently favored by the market:** Company should be stocked with current fashion trends and targeted to consumers' tastes. • **Establishment of brand names:** Recognizable brand names should be stocked. • **Attractive product presentation:** Store layout and product display must encourage product purchase and reinforce a strong company image. • **Experienced workforce:** Companies need to staff an adequate amount to ensure excellent customer service.
Supply and Demand Conditions	The apparel retail industry consists of all menswear, women's wear, and children's wear. The key suppliers or the industry are clothing manufacturers and wholesalers. The fluctuations in the cost of power, dyes, chemicals, and cotton have strengthened supplier power in an industry that relies heavily on the availability of raw materials. Companies in the industry produce apparel in domestic and foreign factories, with more than 80% of industry inputs sourced from international suppliers. Independent third parties manufacture nearly all of our products for us. As a result, we are directly impacted by increases in the cost of those products . For example, cotton prices rose substantially during fiscal 2011, which put significant pressure on our average unit costs and gross margins. If we experience significant increases in demand or need to replace an existing vendor, there can be no assurance that additional manufacturing capacity will be available when required on terms that are acceptable to us or that any vendor would allocate sufficient capacity to us in order to meet our requirements. In addition, for any new manufacturing source, we may encounter delays in production and added costs as a result of the time it takes to train our vendors in our methods, products, quality control standards, and

environmental, labor, health, and safety standards. Moreover, in the event of a significant disruption in the supply of the fabrics or raw materials used by our vendors in the manufacture of our products, our vendors might not be able to locate alternative suppliers of materials of comparable quality at an acceptable price. Any delays, interruption, or increased costs in the manufacture of our products could result in lower sales and net income.

Because independent vendors manufacture nearly all of our products outside of our principal sales markets, third parties must transport our products over large geographic distances. Delays in the shipment or delivery of our products due to the availability of transportation, work stoppages, port strikes, infrastructure congestion, or other factors, and costs and delays associated with transitioning between vendors, could adversely impact our financial performance. Manufacturing delays or unexpected demand for our products may require us to use faster, but more expensive, transportation methods such as aircraft, which could adversely affect our gross margins. In addition, the cost of fuel is a significant component in transportation costs, so increases in the price of petroleum products can adversely affect our gross margins.

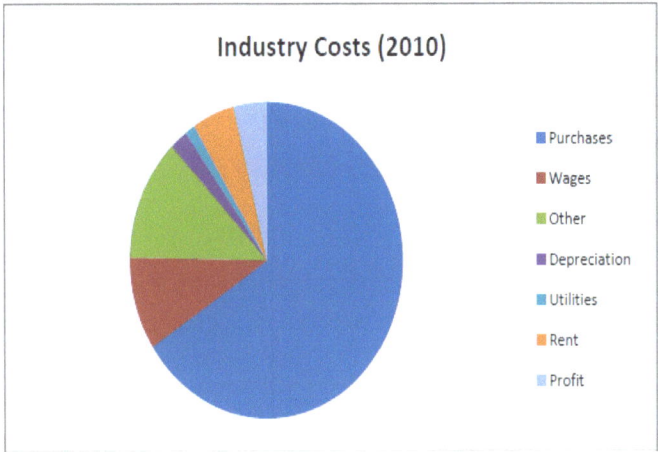

Industry Costs (2010)

- Purchases
- Wages
- Other
- Depreciation
- Utilities
- Rent
- Profit

The chart above illustrates that purchasing cost of materials is the largest expense of the industry, accounting for 65.8% of industry revenue. Clothes sourced from low-cost overseas manufacturers account for 83-92% of the industry's domestic demand.

	Clothing retailers are affected by competition from substitutes such as specialty clothing stores (e.g. women's clothing stores) and internet-based retailers. As consumers buy more clothing from alternative stores, demand for clothing from industry establishments will likely decrease. This driver is expected to increase slowly during 2012, posing a potential threat to the industry. Also, the number of adults in the United States affects demand for family clothing. Stores in this industry retail clothing for all genders and age groups, but adults are the primary purchasers of this clothing; therefore, demand increases as the number of adults aged 20 to 64 rises. This driver is expected to increase slowly during 2012. The typical industry participant experiences the effects of globalization through upstream supply industries. More than 80.0% of industry inputs are sourced from international suppliers, prices for inputs and industry purchasing cost depend on exchange rates, international political relations and tariff rates. A US dollar weakens, as it did through most of the current five year period, internationally sourced inputs become more expensive to the domestic apparel supply chain.
Analysis of stage in life cycle	As part of a fairly established sector and with few opportunities to expand, the Family Clothing Stores industry continues to operate in the mature stage of its life cycle. Its value added (IVA) is expected to grow at 1.8% over the 10 years to 2017, compared to overall annualized GDP growth of 2.1% per year. Because the industry's contribution to the economy (measured via its IVA) is growing at a pace similar to GDP, the industry is exhibiting traits of maturity. The number of firms engaged in family clothes retailing has increased at an average annual rate of 1.3% per year over the five years to 2012, and is expected to grow at an additional 1.2% over the next five years. The expansion of low-priced retailers during the recession has boosted the overall expansion of the industry. During the next five years, IBIS World forecasts that the rebounding consumer sentiment will lead to increased industry

demand. Potential entrants will find it easier to open a family clothing store.

Product segments are well defined, with fashion trends exhibiting little effect on family clothing stores. Children's clothes are primarily purchased out of necessity. Clothes for men and women who have a family are also purchased mainly as needed rather than to follow fashion trends. As such, demand for and innovation of new styles and products is very limited within this industry. The consumers frequenting these stores are also generally the same, with parents dominating the market.

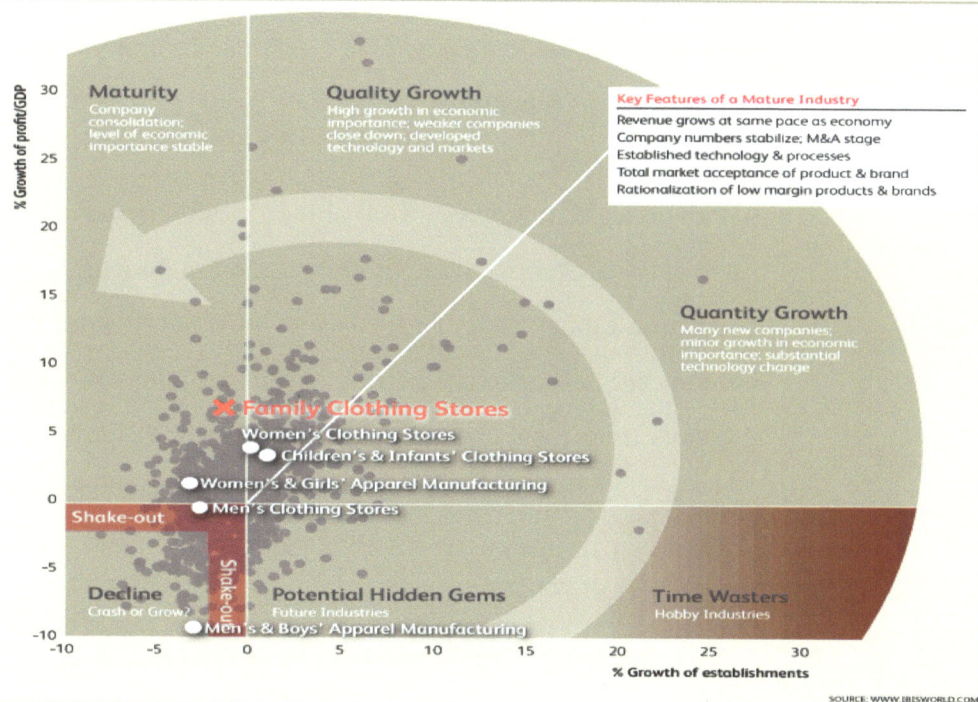

% Growth of profit/GDP

Maturity
Company consolidation; level of economic importance stable

Quality Growth
High growth in economic importance; weaker companies close down; developed technology and markets

Key Features of a Mature Industry
Revenue grows at same pace as economy
Company numbers stabilize; M&A stage
Established technology & processes
Total market acceptance of product & brand
Rationalization of low margin products & brands

Quantity Growth
Many new companies; minor growth in economic importance; substantial technology change

✖ **Family Clothing Stores**
● **Women's Clothing Stores**
● **Children's & Infants' Clothing Stores**
● **Women's & Girls' Apparel Manufacturing**
● **Men's Clothing Stores**

Shake-out

Shake-out

Decline
Crash or Grow?
● **Men's & Boys' Apparel Manufacturing**

Potential Hidden Gems
Future Industries

Time Wasters
Hobby Industries

% Growth of establishments

SOURCE: WWW.IBISWORLD.COM

This chart shows where the industry lies within the three key life cycle stages, growth, maturity or decline, by plotting the relationship between the industry's change in contribution to the economy and the percentage change in the number of industry establishments. To show the industry's relative position in the economy, the life cycle stages of its key supply, demand and competing industries are also shown. Each life cycle stage represents unique

	characteristics that may be used to make strategic decisions and to determine the level of competition and opportunities that may exist. Most industries move counter clockwise around the chart segments: from growth to maturity and then to decline.
Pace of technological change	The level of technology change is low. Technological advances include the use of electronic barcode scanners, automated warehouse equipment and electronic surveillance. Electronic barcode scanning systems enable efficient customer check-out and returns, store-based inventory management and rapid order replenishment. The TJX Companies uses specialized computer inventory planning, purchasing and monitoring systems to price and determine inventory levels. This is all done centrally using satellite-transmitted information.
	With losses incurred as a result of theft, retailers need to use security and loss-prevention systems such as closed circuit TV cameras, source tagging, signature-capture technology (used at the point-of-sale, or POS, terminal for credit card transactions) and fingerprint scanning systems that verify customer identity (to combat check fraud). Abercrombie & Fitch has upgraded its systems to help allocate, plan and source merchandise. Increasing efficiencies in this way results in gross margin gains.
	Radio frequency identification (RFID) technology is being introduced to make existing supply chain processes more efficient. Products are "tagged" with chips that "announce" their identity when hit with a non-line-of-sight electromagnetic field. This assists with forecasting demand and managing inventory levels. RFID technology also provides a variety of possible benefits to consumers. These include faster recovery of stolen items, consumer savings stemming from reduced operating costs, and faster, more reliable product recalls. Some major players are using labor management systems to make better use of their employees. For instance, Ross Stores has a labor

	management system that tracks in-store labor against budget and forecasts to determine if resources are being allocated correctly and if adjustments need to be made. Gap Inc. technology forces involve Gap enhancing the company's distribution centers allowing them to operate more efficiently in the industry. Gap Inc. uses products such as bar coding, e-tailing, interactive kiosks, and electronic data interchange systems to provide efficiency.
Vertical Integration	Although the Gap began by selling Levi's exclusively, its ultimate growth and dominance began once it started to manufacture products under its own label. Vertical integration also allowed Gap to lower transaction costs and reduces supply threats created by Levi's. Gap has used a vertical integration since virtually all aspects of brand development from product design and distribution, to marketing, merchandising and shopping environments are controlled by Gap. The advantage of having a vertical integration is that the company doesn't pay wholesalers and retailers in order to sell its products. Gap Inc. is not a vertically integrated global operation; they will face roadblocks, particularly, in the form of price pressure from vertically integrated global retailers. The disadvantage of not being a global vertically integrated operation has resulted in being slow in time-to-market causing it to miss fashion trends.
Economies of scale	As an early entrant, Gap has been able to take advantage of economies of scale within the industry. Due to the economies of scale, Gap has numerous opportunities of effective inventory management and sourcing. Currently, Gap operates distribution centers in California, Kentucky, Maryland, Ohio and New York within the United States and in Canada, England, and the Netherlands outside the United States. Two distribution centers are attributed solely to fulfill catalog and Internet orders. Gap outsources 100% of its

products from 1,100 suppliers worldwide. Of the merchandise, 80% is produced outside the United States, with China and Hong Kong representing 12% of all goods and 56 other countries for the rest.

Our past performance may not be a reliable indicator of future performance because actual future results and trends may differ materially depending on a variety of factors, including but not limited to the risks and uncertainties discussed below. The Company's performance is subject to global economic conditions and their impact on levels of consumer spending worldwide. Some of the factors influencing consumer spending include higher levels of unemployment, higher consumer debt levels, reductions in net worth based on market declines and uncertainty, home foreclosures and reductions in home values, fluctuating interest rates and credit availability, government austerity measures, fluctuating fuel and other energy costs, fluctuating commodity prices, and general uncertainty regarding the overall future economic environment. Consumer purchases of discretionary items, including our merchandise, generally decline during periods when disposable income is adversely affected or there is economic uncertainty. Adverse changes in the global economy, or in any of the regions in which we sell our products, could reduce consumer confidence, and thereby could negatively affect earnings and have a material adverse effect on our results of operations. For example, the global financial economic downturn that began in 2008 and continued throughout 2011, particularly in Europe, has negatively impacted consumer confidence. In a challenging and uncertain economic environment, we cannot predict whether or when such circumstances may improve or worsen, or what impact, if any, such circumstances could have on our business, results of operations, cash flows, and financial position.

Learning & Experience curve effects	The learning curve is low; the industry is mature with few opportunities to expand and new entrants will find it easy to open a family clothing store. Product segments are well defined.

Barriers to entry	Barriers to entry in this industry are medium and are steady. The high costs involved in developing and maintaining brand reputations provide a major barrier to entry in this industry. As existing players have already established brand names in respective product offerings, new entrants will have to invest money and time before consumers shift away from strong brand names and purchase relatively new brands. Due to the recent economic slowdown, consumer demand has shifted toward more competitively priced clothing. Family clothing stores have catered to these demands by providing branded merchandise at discounted prices. Existing stores, such as TJX and Ross Stores, are able to offer merchandise at discounted prices by purchasing products earlier in the season at low prices through established sourcing networks. New entrants do not have access to these established networks, so selling merchandise at discounted prices may decrease profit margins. **Barriers to Entry checklist** **Level** Competition High Concentration Low Life Cycle Stage Mature Capital Intensity Medium Technology Change Low Regulation & Policy Medium Industry Assistance Low SOURCE: WWW.IBISWORLD.COM
Regulation & Deregulation	The Regulation level within the Family Clothing Store Industry is classified as medium. Congress and states enact trade regulations to maintain a free and competitive economy. Congress has passed the Sherman Act, the Wilson Act, the Clayton Act and the Robinson-Patman Act regarding unfair competition. Together these make up US federal antitrust law. The Sherman Act (1890) prohibits the formation of monopolies that hinder competition. The Wilson Act (1895) prohibits conspiracies that restrain import trade. The Clayton Act (1914) bans certain forms of price discrimination. Finally, the Robinson-Patman Act (1936) provides some protection to small independent retailers and their suppliers from unfair

competition from vertically integrated, multi-location chain stores. States have enacted their own antitrust laws to ensure that the public is provided with the best prices, quality and competition among businesses, including women's clothing stores.

The laws that affect credit programs offered by retailers include the Federal Consumer Credit Protection Act (Truth in Lending) which specifies written disclosure of information relating to financing. For example, the annual percentage rate is required to be revealed. The Federal Fair Credit Reporting Act specifies that certain disclosures to potential customers concerning credit information can be used to deny credit. The Federal Equal Credit Opportunity Act prohibits discriminating against any credit applicants based on certain grounds. The Fair Debt Collection Practices Act regulates how payments are collected on credit accounts. Finally, the Gramm-Leach-Bliley Act requires retailers to disclose their privacy policy as it relates to customers' non-public personal information.

Trade restrictions, including increased tariffs or quotas, embargoes, safeguards, and customs restrictions against apparel items, as well as U.S. or foreign labor strikes, work stoppages, or boycotts, could increase the cost or reduce the supply of apparel available to us and adversely affect our business, financial condition, and results of operations. We cannot predict whether any of the countries in which our merchandise currently is manufactured or may be manufactured in the future will be subject to additional trade restrictions imposed by the U.S. and other foreign governments, including the likelihood, type, or effect of any such restrictions. In addition, we face the possibility of anti-dumping or countervailing duties lawsuits from U.S. domestic producers. We are unable to determine the impact of the changes to the quota system or the impact that potential tariff lawsuits could have on our global sourcing operations. Our sourcing operations may be adversely affected by trade limits

	or political and financial instability, resulting in the disruption of trade from exporting countries, significant fluctuation in the value of the U.S. dollar against foreign currencies, restrictions on the transfer of funds, and/or other trade disruptions.
Globalization	Globalization in this industry is low and the trend is steady. The Family Clothing Stores industry is comprised of a large number of small companies; over 80.0% of firms operating within the industry employ four or fewer people, so no single company owns a substantial portion of the market. Additionally, the major companies in this industry are all domestically owned. However, the Gap generates about 12.0% of its total revenue from international markets and the TJX Corporation generates about 15.0% of its sales from international markets. These numbers are still relatively small compared with overall revenue, giving the industry a low level of globalization. The typical industry participant experiences the effects of globalization through upstream supply industries. Because more than 80.0% of industry inputs are sourced from international suppliers, prices for inputs and industry purchasing costs depend on exchange rates, international political relations and tariff rates. As the US dollar weakens, as it did through much of the current five-year period, internationally sourced inputs become more expensive to the domestic apparel supply chain.
Trends	In recent years The Gap, Inc. has experienced decreasing in-store sales in the United States as a result of the recession and an increase in online sales. This trend mainly affects the Gap brand but the decreases in same-store sales have become less severe and we expect The Gap, Inc. to experience modest growth in the United States beginning in 2011.

Current economic trends such as GDP, consumer sentiment, and disposable income indicate optimism in the apparel retail industry and we expect annual growth of 2.6% for the industry over the next five years.

The current trend toward value-line clothing is shifting to more expensive lines as the economy recovers from the previous recession.

Internet shopping has changed the retail business by making it easy to navigate between many brands, categories, and products quickly. Consumers can also quickly determine whether a desired product is being sold by a competitor for a lower price. We expect that the trend of consumers shifting to purchasing online will continue and online retail sales will grow by 10% in 2011 and maintain this growth through 2014. The Direct Reportable Segment of The Gap, Inc. includes all online sales for the company. Growth in this segment has been strong due to increasing popularity over the past five years and we expect
this trend to continue.

Apparel retail sales are driven by demographic trends. Changing fashion trends among women and teens result in short product life cycles. Age distribution, ethnicity, gender, and priorities force retailers to establish a narrow target market, stressing the importance of brand recognition. The Gap, Inc.'s increase in Asian same-store sales is in response to the growth opportunities presented by the Asian market. We expect this trend to continue as the market is unsaturated and demand has not yet been fully met.

G. Organizational Structure:

1. Type

Organizational structures can be "tall," illustrating many tiers between the common workers or they can be "flat," meaning there are very few levels between the common worker and the owner. Gap, Inc. consists of a flat organization structure with two levels of management. Additionally, Gap's internal structure organization system is to support the company's goal of specific identities for each of the clothing-brand lines. The company divided its subordinates as product base with brands that are under GAP (such as Banana Republic, Old Navy, Gap, Piperlime and Athleta) and GAP itself (North America, Europe, Asia). Each brand was charged with maintaining complete control of its product through a highly vertically-integrated corporate structure. These product based departments resemble a matrix structure of a firm due to the collaboration between multi-skilled individuals with diverse backgrounds and unique knowledge to produce the final product for the brand. Keep in mind, Gap established an International unit. While the division was treated as a profit center, it was a channel-based division, rather than a brand division.GAP Inc. is a decentralized company. Although we could only see a few members in the organizational structure, we know that the ones at the second level of managements are all head of a department of brand. Therefore, it is obvious, daily decision making does not often reach the highest levels of hierarchy. Supporting activities includes the following components: company infrastructure, information systems, materials management, and human resource.

Gap, Inc. Organizational Structure

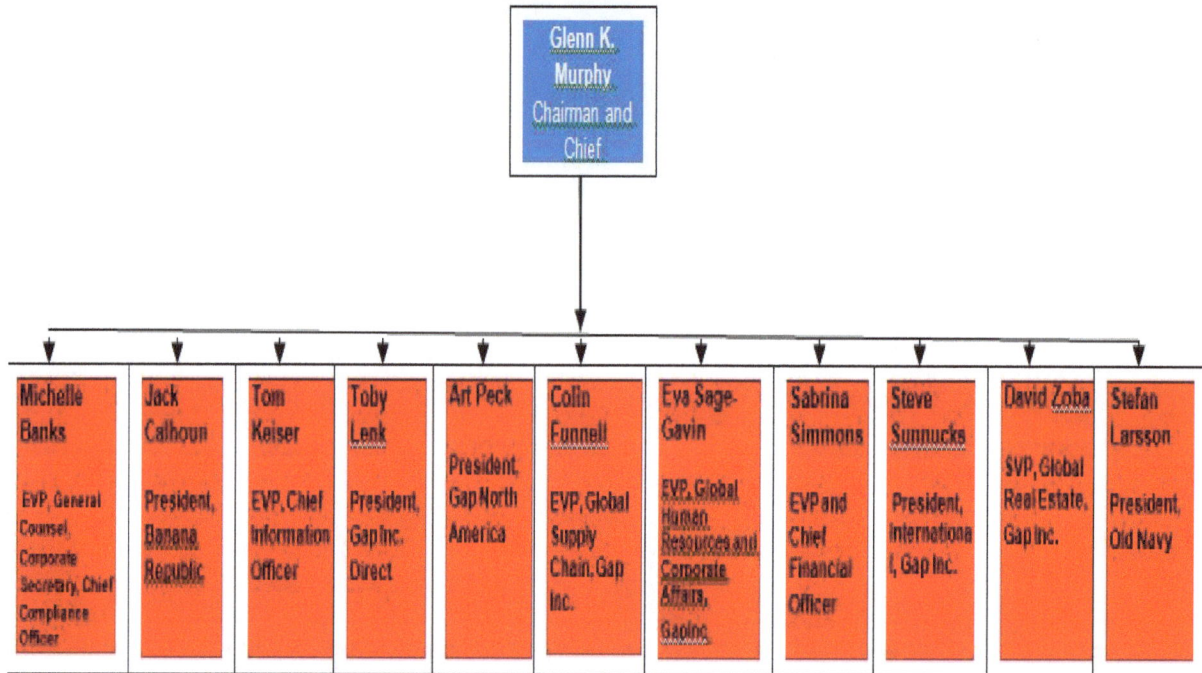

Michelle Banks	Jack Calhoun	Tom Keiser	Toby Lenk	Art Peck	Colin Funnell	Eva Sage-Gavin	Sabrina Simmons	Steve Sunnucks	David Zoba	Stefan Larsson
EVP, General Counsel, Corporate Secretary, Chief Compliance Officer	President, Banana Republic	EVP, Chief Information Officer	President, Gap Inc. Direct	President, Gap North America	EVP, Global Supply Chain, Gap Inc.	EVP, Global Human Resources and Corporate Affairs, Gap Inc.	EVP and Chief Financial Officer	President, International, Gap Inc.	SVP, Global Real Estate, Gap Inc.	President, Old Navy

Gap, Inc Operating Business Units

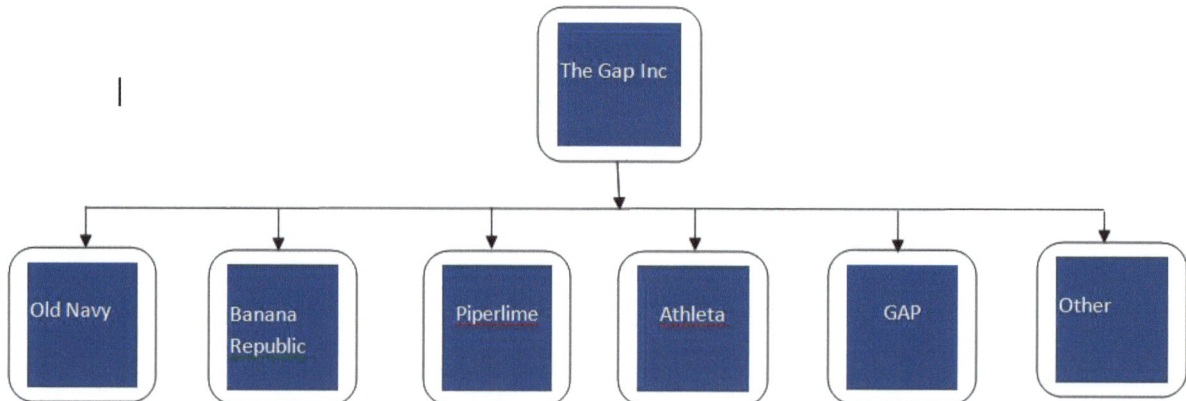

The Gap Inc

Old Navy | Banana Republic | Piperlime | Athleta | GAP | Other

2. Advantages and Disadvantages

The advantage of a two tier leads to open communication channels between employers and employees. Gap, Inc. uses a variety mix in building the base of structure for the firm by dividing its structure based on product, human resource and finance. The HR and the finance sector are classified as a separate department so each department can be compared easily with statistics. It appears that Gap uses a divisional organization structure. According to www.smallbusiness.com, a divisional organization structure is defined as "a divisional structure usually consists of several parallel teams focusing on a single product or service line". Gap, Inc has one set of executives to handle such things as finance, information technology, human resources, etc, but it has company President's for its divisions, which are categorized by brand and/or geographic location. There are advantages to having a decentralize organization such as it encourages lower level management and employees to exercise initiative, act responsibly, promote motivation and involvement. However, disadvantages occur when the organization is put at risk when bad decisions are implemented and impedes cross-business coordination.

H. Financial Analysis/Altman and DuPont

1. Graphs

The financial figures below were used to generate and analyze the following graphs

GAP, INC. (GPS) Cash Flow BALANCE SHEET

Fiscal year ends in January. USD in millions except per share data.

	2008-01	2009-01	2010-01	2011-01	2012-01
Assets					
Current assets					
Cash					
Cash and cash equivalents	1724	1715	2348	1561	1885
Short-term investments	177		225	100	

Total cash	1901	1715	2573	1661	1885
Receivables				205	297
Inventories	1575	1506	1477	1620	1615
Deferred income taxes			193	190	
Prepaid expenses			260	145	
Other current assets	610	784	161	105	512
Total current assets	4086	4005	4664	3926	4309
Non-current assets					
Property, plant and equipment					
Land	1022	988	1086	1093	1096
Fixtures and equipment	2401	2377	3249	3340	3423
Other properties	3897	3880	3092	3140	3264
Property and equipment, at cost	7320	7245	7427	7573	7783
Accumulated Depreciation	-4053	-4312	-4799	-5010	-5260
Property, plant and equipment, net	3267	2933	2628	2563	2523
Goodwill			99	99	99
Intangible assets			61	57	77
Other long-term assets	485	626	533	420	414
Total non-current assets	3752	3559	3321	3139	3113
Total assets	7838	7564	7985	7065	7422
Liabilities and stockholders' equity					
Liabilities					
Current liabilities					
Short-term debt	138	50			59
Accounts payable	1006	975	1027	1049	1066
Taxes payable				50	5
Accrued liabilities	410	1076	1063	996	395
Other current liabilities	879	57			603
Total current liabilities	2433	2158	2131	2095	2128
Non-current liabilities					

Long-term debt	50			890	1606
Capital leases					933
Other long-term liabilities	1081	1019	963		
Total non-current liabilities	1131	1019	963	890	2539
Total liabilities	3564	3177	3094	2985	4667
Stockholders' equity					
Common stock	55	55	55	55	55
Additional paid-in capital	2783	2895	2935	2939	2867
Retained earnings	9223	9947	10815	11767	12364
Treasury stock	-7912	-8633	-9069	-10866	-12760
Accumulated comprehensive income	125	123	155	185	229
Total stockholders' equity	4274	4387	4891	4080	2755
Total liabilities & stockholders' equity	7838	7564	7985	7065	7422

Growth Profitability and Financial Ratios for Gap, Inc.

Financials

	2008-01	2009-01	2010-01	2011-01	2012-01
Revenue USD Mil	15,763	14,526	14,197	14,664	14,549
Gross Margin %	36.1	37.5	40.3	40.2	36.2
Operating Income USD Mil	1,315	1,548	1,815	1,968	1,438
Operating Margin %	8.3	10.7	12.8	13.4	9.9
Net Income USD Mil	833	967	1,102	1,204	833
Earnings Per Share USD	1.05	1.34	1.58	1.88	1.56
Dividends USD	0.32	0.34	0.34	0.4	0.45
Payout Ratio %	29.4	25.4	21.5	21.3	28.8

Shares Mil	794	719	699	641	533
Book Value Per Share USD	5.69	6.21	7.09	6.94	5.68
Operating Cash Flow USD Mil	2,081	1,412	1,928	1,744	1,363
Cap Spending USD Mil	-682	-431	-334	-557	-548
Free Cash Flow USD Mil	1,399	981	1,594	1,187	815
Free Cash Flow Per Share USD	1.76	1.34	2.27	1.85	1.53
Working Capital USD Mil	1,653	1,847	2,533	1,831	2,181

Key Ratios -> Profitability

Margins % of Sales	2008-01	2009-01	2010-01	2011-01	2012-01
Revenue	100	100	100	100	100
COGS	63.89	62.5	59.68	59.84	63.75
Gross Margin	36.11	37.5	40.32	40.16	36.25
SG&A					
R&D					
Other	27.77	26.84	27.53	26.74	26.37
Operating Margin	8.34	10.66	12.78	13.42	9.88
Net Int Inc & Other	0.58	0.25	0.01	0.1	-0.47
EBT Margin	8.92	10.9	12.79	13.52	9.41

Profitability	2008-01	2009-01	2010-01	2011-01	2012-01
Tax Rate %	38.34	38.95	39.32	39.25	39.15
Net Margin %	5.28	6.66	7.76	8.21	5.73
Asset Turnover (Average)	1.92	1.89	1.83	1.95	2.01
Return on Assets %	10.17	12.56	14.17	16	11.5

Financial Leverage (Average)	1.83	1.72	1.63	1.73	2.69
Return on Equity %	17.63	22.33	23.76	26.84	24.37
Return on Invested Capital %	16.42	21.86	23.63	22.4	16.05

Key Ratios -> Growth

	2008-01	2009-01	2010-01	2011-01	2012-01
Revenue %					
Year over Year	-1	-7.85	-2.26	3.29	-0.78
3-Year Average	-1.04	-3.21	-3.75	-2.38	0.05
5-Year Average	1.75	-1.73	-2.69	-1.76	-1.81
10-Year Average	9.25	4.84	2.01	0.7	0.5
Operating Income %					
Year over Year	7.35	17.72	17.25	8.43	-26.93
3-Year Average	-14.24	-4.46	14	14.38	-2.43
5-Year Average	5.36	-3.8	-2.74	2.43	4.14
10-Year Average	4.44	1.51	-0.01	3.14	15.6
Net Income %					
Year over Year	7.07	16.09	13.96	9.26	-30.81
3-Year Average	-10.19	-4.58	12.31	13.06	-4.85
5-Year Average	11.77	-1.25	-0.85	1.58	1.38
10-Year Average	4.55	1.61	-0.23	3.21	
EPS %					
Year over Year	12.9	27.62	17.91	18.99	-17.02
3-Year Average	-4.62	2.62	19.32	21.43	5.2
5-Year Average	14.22	4.22	5.48	8.68	10.9
10-Year Average	6.16	3.95	2.29	6.52	

Liquidity/Financial Health

	2008-01	2009-01	2010-01	2011-01	2012-01
Current Ratio	1.68	1.86	2.19	1.87	2.02
Quick Ratio	0.78	0.79	1.21	0.89	1.03
Financial Leverage	1.83	1.72	1.63	1.73	2.69
Debt/Equity	0.01			0.22	0.92

Key Ratios -> Efficiency Ratios

Efficiency	2008-01	2009-01	2010-01	2011-01	2012-01
Days Sales Outstanding				5.1	6.3
Days Inventory	61.09	61.93	64.25	64.41	63.65
Payables Period	38.33	39.82	43.12	43.18	41.62
Cash Conversion Cycle				26.34	28.33
Receivables Turnover				71.53	57.96
Inventory Turnover	5.98	5.89	5.68	5.67	5.73
Fixed Assets Turnover	4.88	4.69	5.11	5.65	5.72
Asset Turnover	1.92	1.89	1.83	1.95	2.01

ROSS STORES, INC. (ROST)

CashFlow BALANCE SHEET

Fiscal year ends in January. USD in

millions except per share data.

	2008-01	2009-01	2010-01	2011-01	2012-01
Assets					
Current assets					

Cash					
Cash and cash equivalents	258	321	768	834	650
Short-term investments	6	1	2	3	1
Total cash	264	322	770	837	650
Receivables	37	41	44	45	51
Inventories	1025	881	872	1087	1130
Deferred income taxes	20	14		10	6
Prepaid expenses	52	55	59	64	87
Total current assets	1398	1314	1745	2043	1924
Non-current assets					
Property, plant and equipment					
Land	141	201	240	241	338
Fixtures and equipment	942	1074	1190	1259	1409
Other properties	572	583	559	654	789
Property and equipment, at cost	1654	1858	1988	2153	2536
Accumulated Depreciation	-786	-907	-1045	-1170	-1294
Property, plant and equipment, net	868	952	943	984	1242
Equity and other investments		38	17	14	6
Goodwill	3	3	3	3	3
Intangible assets	10	8			
Other long-term assets	92	41	60	72	127
Total non-current assets	973	1042	1023	1073	1377
Total assets	2371	2356	2769	3116	3301
Liabilities and stockholders' equity					
Liabilities					
Current liabilities					
Accounts payable	637	537	658	767	762

Deferred income taxes			3		
Taxes payable		9	52	58	31
Accrued liabilities	352	409	478	527	553
Other current liabilities	22				
Total current liabilities	1011	955	1191	1352	1346
Non-current liabilities					
Long-term debt	150	150	150	150	150
Deferred taxes liabilities	79	97	96	91	109
Other long-term liabilities	161	157	175	190	204
Total non-current liabilities	390	404	421	431	462
Total liabilities	1401	1359	1611	1784	1808
Stockholders' equity					
Common stock	1	1	1	1	2
Additional paid-in capital	578	626	682	741	789
Retained earnings	416	401	511	637	763
Treasury stock	-26	-31	-37	-46	-62
Accumulated other comprehensive income	1	-1	0	0	1
Total stockholders' equity	971	996	1157	1333	1493
Total liabilities and stockholders' equity	2371	2356	2769	3116	3301

Growth Profitability and Financial Ratios for Ross Stores, Inc.

Financials

	2008-01	2009-01	2010-01	2011-01	2012-01
Revenue USD Mil	5,975	6,486	7,184	7,866	8,608
Gross Margin %	22.7	23.6	25.8	27.2	27.5
Operating Income USD Mil	421	495	726	907	1,053

Operating Margin %	7	7.6	10.1	11.5	12.2
Net Income USD Mil	261	305	443	555	657
Earnings Per Share USD	0.95	1.17	1.77	2.32	2.86
Dividends USD	0.15	0.19	0.22	0.32	0.44
Payout Ratio %	15.8	16.3	12.4	13.8	15.4
Shares Mil	274	263	250	240	230
Book Value Per Share USD	3.58	3.79	4.67	5.64	6.58
Operating Cash Flow USD Mil	354	583	888	673	820
Cap Spending USD Mil	-236	-224	-158	-199	-416
Free Cash Flow USD Mil	117	359	730	474	404
Free Cash Flow Per Share USD	0.43	1.35	2.89	1.98	1.76
Working Capital USD Mil	387	358	555	691	578

Key Ratios -> Profitability

Margins % of Sales	2008-01	2009-01	2010-01	2011-01	2012-01
Revenue	100	100	100	100	100
COGS	77.29	76.42	74.15	72.84	72.5
Gross Margin	22.71	23.58	25.85	27.16	27.5
SG&A	15.66	15.95	15.74	15.63	15.15
R&D					
Other					0.12
Operating Margin	7.05	7.63	10.11	11.53	12.23

Net Int Inc & Other	0.07		-0.11	-0.12	
EBT Margin	7.11	7.64	10	11.4	12.23

Profitability	2008-01	2009-01	2010-01	2011-01	2012-01
Tax Rate %	38.59	38.34	38.38	38.15	37.6
Net Margin %	4.37	4.71	6.16	7.05	7.63
Asset Turnover (Average)	2.53	2.74	2.8	2.67	2.68
Return on Assets %	11.04	12.92	17.28	18.86	20.48
Financial Leverage (Average)	2.44	2.36	2.39	2.34	2.21
Return on Equity %	27.76	31.06	41.12	44.56	46.51
Return on Invested Capital %	23.94	26.95	36.09	39.77	42.05

Key Ratios -> Growth					
	2008-01	2009-01	2010-01	2011-01	2012-01
Revenue %					
Year over Year	7.27	8.55	10.76	9.49	9.44
3-Year Average	12.11	9.47	8.85	9.6	9.89
5-Year Average	11.09	10.59	11.12	9.73	9.1
10-Year Average	11.63	11.51	11.27	11.25	11.17
Operating Income %					
Year over Year	8.07	17.6	46.63	23.54	17.4
3-Year Average	12.5	15.02	23.06	28.67	28.6
5-Year Average	4.96	5.76	19.68	22.74	22
10-Year Average	7.97	8.47	11.02	13.63	15.11
Net Income %					
Year over Year	8.04	17	44.96	25.31	18.45
3-Year Average	15.39	15.23	22.37	28.57	29.1
5-Year Average	5.35	6.01	21.11	22.68	22.15

10-Year Average	8.31	8.6	11.42	13.84	15.54
EPS %					
Year over Year	11.76	22.63	51.93	30.79	23.54
3-Year Average	18.91	19.66	27.7	34.57	34.9
5-Year Average	8.56	9.65	25.66	27.76	27.46
10-Year Average	12.45	12.78	15.75	17.67	19.6

Liquidity/Financial Health	2008-01	2009-01	2010-01	2011-01	2012-01
Current Ratio	1.38	1.38	1.47	1.51	1.43
Quick Ratio	0.3	0.38	0.68	0.65	0.52
Financial Leverage	2.44	2.36	2.39	2.34	2.21
Debt/Equity	0.15	0.15	0.13	0.11	0.1

Key Ratios -> Efficiency Ratios

Efficiency	2008-01	2009-01	2010-01	2011-01	2012-01
Days Sales Outstanding	2.06	2.21	2.17	2.08	2.04
Days Inventory	82.08	70.19	60.07	62.41	64.83
Payables Period	52.76	43.22	40.94	45.41	44.72
Cash Conversion Cycle	31.38	29.18	21.3	19.08	22.15
Receivables Turnover	176.85	164.96	168.24	175.55	178.91
Inventory Turnover	4.45	5.2	6.08	5.85	5.63
Fixed Assets Turnover	7.39	7.13	7.58	8.17	7.74
Asset Turnover	2.53	2.74	2.8	2.67	2.68

TJX COMPANIES (TJX) Cash Flow BALANCE SHEET

Fiscal year ends in January. USD in millions except per share data.

	2008-	2009-	2010-01	2011-01	2012-

	01	01			01
Assets					
Current assets					
Cash					
Cash and cash equivalents	733	454	1615	1742	1507
Short-term investments			131	76	95
Total cash	733	454	1745	1818	1602
Receivables	143	144	148	200	204
Inventories	2737	2619	2532	2765	2951
Deferred income taxes	163	136	122	66	106
Prepaid expenses	216	274	256	250	270
Total current assets	3992	3626	4804	5100	5133
Non-current assets					
Property, plant and equipment					
Land	278	280	282	321	350
Fixtures and equipment	2675	2784	3087	3256	3427
Other properties	1818	1761	1964	2123	2344
Property and equipment, at cost	4771	4826	5332	5700	6121
Accumulated Depreciation	-2536	-2624	-3045	-3239	-3406
Property, plant and equipment, net	2235	2201	2287	2461	2715
Goodwill	182	180	72	72	180
Intangible assets			108	108	
Other long-term assets	191	171	193	232	254
Total non-current assets	2608	2552	2660	2872	3149
Total assets	6600	6178	7464	7972	8282
Liabilities and stockholders' equity					
Liabilities					
Current liabilities					
Short-term debt	2	395			
Capital leases			2	3	3

Accounts payable	1517	1276	1508	1684	1645
Taxes payable			137	99	50
Accrued liabilities	919	756	1248	1348	1365
Other current liabilities	323	341			
Total current liabilities	2761	2768	2895	3133	3063
Non-current liabilities					
Long-term debt	833	366	774	774	774
Capital leases	20	18	16	13	10
Deferred taxes liabilities	43	127	192	242	363
Other long-term liabilities	811	765	697	709	862
Total non-current liabilities	1708	1276	1680	1739	2009
Total liabilities	4469	4044	4575	4872	5072
Stockholders' equity					
Common stock	428	413	409	390	747
Retained earnings	1732	1940	2614	2802	2655
Accumulated other comprehensive income	-29	-218	-134	-92	-193
Total stockholders' equity	2131	2135	2889	3100	3209
Total liabilities and stockholders' equity	6600	6178	7464	7972	8282

Growth Profitability and Financial Ratios for TJX Companies

Financials

	2008-01	2009-01	2010-01	2011-01	2012-01
Revenue USD Mil	18,647	19,000	20,288	21,942	23,191
Gross Margin %	24.5	24.2	26.2	26.9	27.3
Operating Income USD Mil	1,241	1,465	1,952	2,203	2,411
Operating Margin %	6.7	7.7	9.6	10	10.4

Net Income USD Mil	772	881	1,214	1,343	1,496
Earnings Per Share USD	0.83	1	1.42	1.65	1.93
Dividends USD	0.18	0.17	0.24	0.29	0.55
Payout Ratio %	21.7	15.9	16.6	17.3	28.5
Shares Mil	936	885	855	813	774
Book Value Per Share USD	2.49	2.56	3.44	3.98	4.3
Operating Cash Flow USD Mil	1,361	1,155	2,272	1,976	1,916
Cap Spending USD Mil	-527	-583	-429	-707	-803
Free Cash Flow USD Mil	834	572	1,843	1,269	1,113
Free Cash Flow Per Share USD	0.89	0.64	2.14	1.56	1.44
Working Capital USD Mil	1,231	858	1,909	1,966	2,069

Key Ratios -> Profitability

Margins % of Sales	2008-01	2009-01	2010-01	2011-01	2012-01
Revenue	100	100	100	100	100
COGS	75.52	75.76	73.78	73.1	72.67
Gross Margin	24.48	24.24	26.22	26.9	27.33
SG&A	17.82	16.52	16.41	16.91	16.77
R&D					
Other			0.19	-0.05	0.15
Operating Margin	6.66	7.71	9.62	10.04	10.4
Net Int Inc & Other	0.01	-0.08		-0.18	
EBT Margin	6.66	7.64	9.62	9.86	10.4

Profitability	2008-01	2009-01	2010-01	2011-01	2012-01
Tax Rate %	37.9	36.95	37.82	38.1	37.96
Net Margin %	4.14	4.63	5.98	6.12	6.45

Asset Turnover (Average)	2.94	2.97	2.97	2.84	2.85
Return on Assets %	12.17	13.78	17.79	17.4	18.41
Financial Leverage (Average)	3.1	2.89	2.58	2.57	2.58
Return on Equity %	34.91	41.29	48.31	44.85	47.43
Return on Invested Capital %	25.36	29.85	36.8	35.48	37.94

Key Ratios -> Growth

	2008-01	2009-01	2010-01	2011-01	2012-01
Revenue %					
Year over Year	7.21	3.61	6.78	8.15	5.69
3-Year Average	7.26	5.99	5.86	6.17	6.87
5-Year Average	9.25	7.35	6.35	6.44	5.91
10-Year Average	9.7	9.1	8.72	8.64	8.03
Operating Income %					
Year over Year	-1.66	15.29	37.23	8.69	11.43
3-Year Average	7.41	11.81	15.87	19.81	18.45
5-Year Average	5.2	5.99	12.04	16.22	13.82
10-Year Average	8.95	7.58	8.52	9.51	10.36
Net Income %					
Year over Year	4.57	14.11	37.81	10.68	11.39
3-Year Average	8.17	8.45	18.03	20.29	19.32
5-Year Average	5.94	5.99	12.81	14.24	15.18
10-Year Average	9.74	7.58	8.81	9.58	11.57
EPS %					
Year over Year	7.1	20.48	42	16.2	16.97
3-Year Average	8.49	12.36	22.37	25.74	24.5
5-Year Average	8.78	9.34	16.92	18.54	20.02
10-Year Average	14.33	12.16	13.16	13.5	15.67

Liquidity/Financial Health

	2008-01	2009-01	2010-01	2011-01	2012-01
Current Ratio	1.45	1.31	1.66	1.63	1.68
Quick Ratio	0.32	0.22	0.65	0.64	0.59
Financial Leverage	3.1	2.89	2.58	2.57	2.58
Debt/Equity	0.4	0.18	0.27	0.25	0.24

Key Ratios -> Efficiency Ratios

Efficiency	2008-01	2009-01	2010-01	2011-01	2012-01
Days Sales Outstanding	2.53	2.75	2.62	2.9	3.18
Days Inventory	68.94	67.91	62.81	60.28	61.89
Payables Period	37.44	35.41	33.94	36.31	36.05
Cash Conversion Cycle	34.02	35.26	31.49	26.86	29.03
Receivables Turnover	144.25	132.5	139.14	126.01	114.68
Inventory Turnover	5.29	5.37	5.81	6.06	5.9
Fixed Assets Turnover	8.73	8.57	9.04	9.24	8.96
Asset Turnover	2.94	2.97	2.97	2.84	2.85

Formulas

> **Current Ratio** = Current Assets/Current Liabilities

> **Asset Turonver** = Revenue / Assets

> **Debt-To-Equity Ratio** = Total Liabilities / Shareholders' Equity

> **Accounts Recievable Turnover** = Net Credit Sales / Average Accounts Receivale

> **Inventory Turnover** = Sales / Inventroy or Cost of Goods Sold / Average Inventory

> **Asset Turnover** = Revenue/ Assets

> **Gross Profit Margin** = Revenue- COGS / Revenue

> **Operating Margin** = Operating Income / Net Sales

> **Profit Margin Ratio** = Net Profit before taxes / Sales

- **Net Profit Margin**= Net Profit (After Taxes) / Net Sales X 100
- **Return on Assets**= Net Income / Total Assets
- **Return on Equity** = Net Profit / Average Shareholder Equity for Period

Our success depends in part on our ability to improve sales, in particular at our largest brands. A variety of factors affect comparable sales, including fashion trends, competition, current economic conditions, the timing of new merchandise releases and promotional events, changes in our merchandise mix, the success of marketing programs, and weather conditions. These factors may cause our comparable sales results to differ materially from prior periods and from expectations. Our comparable sales, including the associated comparable online sales, have fluctuated significantly in the past on an annual, quarterly, and monthly basis. Over the past 24 months, our reported monthly comparable sales have ranged from an increase of 11 percent in March 2010 to a decrease of 10 percent in March 2011. Over the past five years, our reported gross margins have ranged from a high of 40.3 percent in fiscal 2009 to a low of 36.1 percent in fiscal 2007. In addition, over the past five years, our reported operating margins have ranged from a high of 13.4 percent in fiscal 2010 to a low of 8.3 percent in fiscal 2007. Our ability to deliver strong comparable sales results and margins depends in large part on accurately forecasting demand and fashion trends, selecting effective marketing techniques, providing an appropriate mix of merchandise for our broad and diverse customer base, managing inventory effectively, using effective pricing strategies, and optimizing store performance. Failure to meet the expectations of investors, securities analysts, or credit rating agencies in one or more future periods could reduce the market price of our common stock and cause our credit ratings to decline.

Revenue Comparison

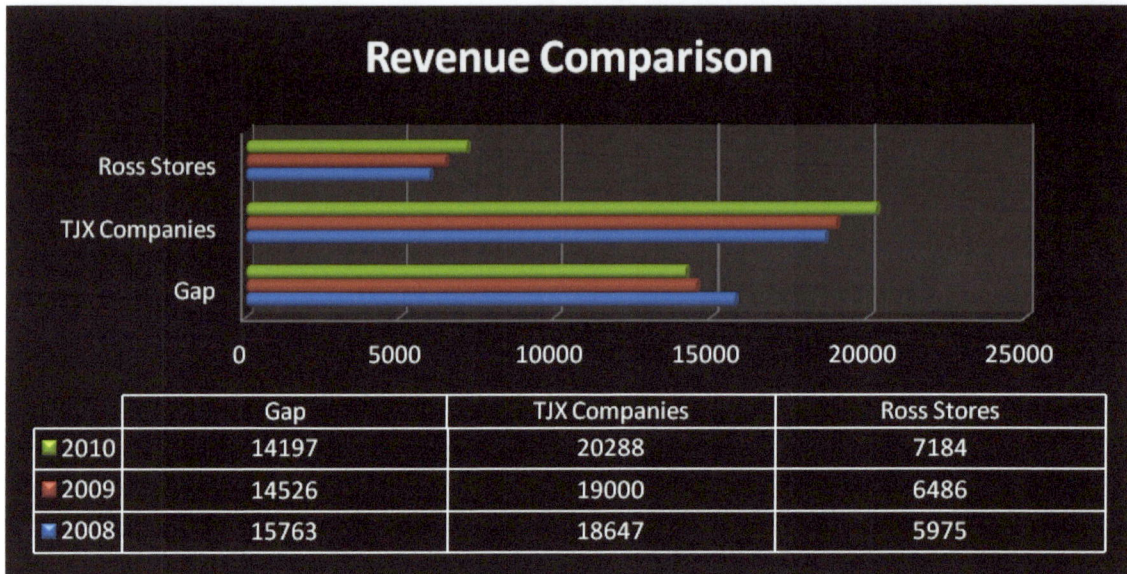

Revenue Comparison

	Gap	TJX Companies	Ross Stores
2010	14197	20288	7184
2009	14526	19000	6486
2008	15763	18647	5975

Revenue can be defined as the amount of money a company actually receives over a specific period; it accounts for sales discounts and deductions for returned merchandise. It is the "top line" or "gross income" figure from which costs are subtracted to determine net income. Revenue is calculated by multiplying the price at which goods or services are sold by the number of units or amount sold.

The financial figures represented above are in USD millions. TJX Companies generate a higher revenue then Gap and Ross Stores. Nevertheless, Gap, Inc. generates larger revenue in comparison with Ross Stores. On the other hand, Gap has been decreasing in revenue since 2008 while Ross Stores and TJX Companies have been steadily increasing despite the economic downturn.

Long Term Debt Comparison

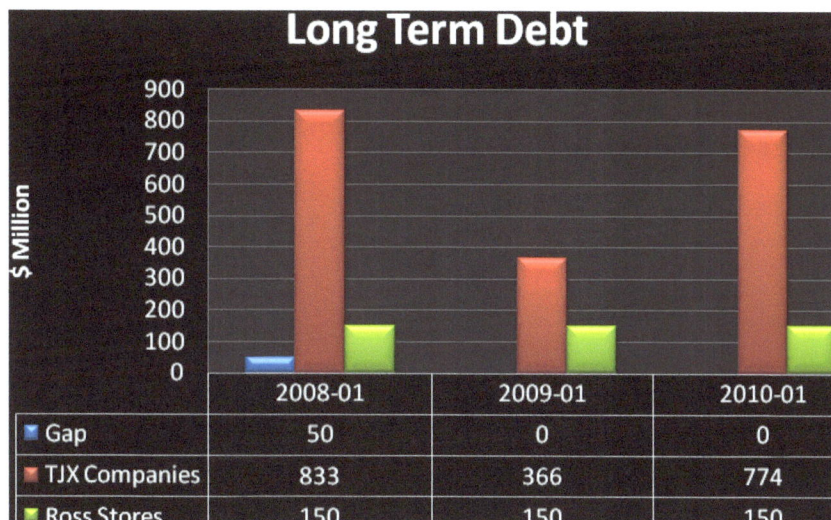

Long Term Debt

	2008-01	2009-01	2010-01
Gap	50	0	0
TJX Companies	833	366	774
Ross Stores	150	150	150

Long-term debt for a company would include any financing or leasing obligations that are to come due in a greater than 12-month period. Such obligations would include company bond issues or long-term leases that have been capitalized on a firm's balance sheet.

Gap, Inc. maintains the minimum long term debt financial figures among its competitors. TJX companies maintain the highest amount for long term debt. Despite decreasing their value from 833 M to 366 M in FY 2009, they witnessed a large jump to 774 M in FY 2010. Gap, Inc. has been decreasing their long term debt continuously throughout FY 2008-2010 while Ross Stores maintained the same amount.

Liquidity Ratios

Current Ratio

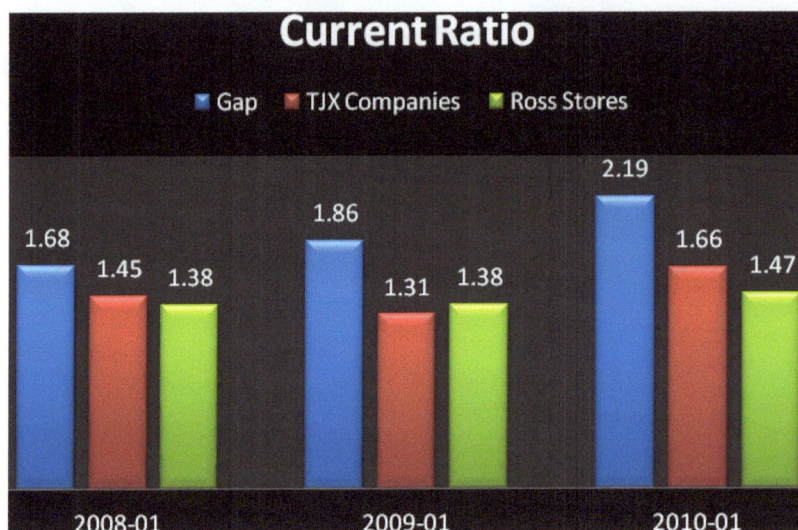

Current Ratio

Gap ■ TJX Companies ■ Ross Stores

	2008-01	2009-01	2010-01
Gap	1.68	1.86	2.19
TJX Companies	1.45	1.31	1.66
Ross Stores	1.38	1.38	1.47

The current ratio measures a company's ability to pay short-term debts and other current liabilities by comparing current assets to current liabilities. The ratio illustrates a company's ability to remain solvent. A current ratio of one means that book value of current assets is exactly the same as book value of current liabilities. In general, investors look for a company with a current ratio of 2:1, meaning current assets twice as large as current liabilities.

All three companies do not represent a current ratio less than one and are in good standing of meeting short-term financial obligations. Gap, Inc's current ratio as of FY 2010 increased compared with FY 2008 and FY 2009 mainly due to its accrued expenses and other current liabilities. Compared to the competition, Gap Inc. has a higher ratio. From FY 2008 to FY 2010, only one company saw a slight decrease in current ratio; TJX Companies noticed a decrease in FY 2009 mainly due to a decrease in cash and cash equivalents and short-term investments.

Quick Ratio

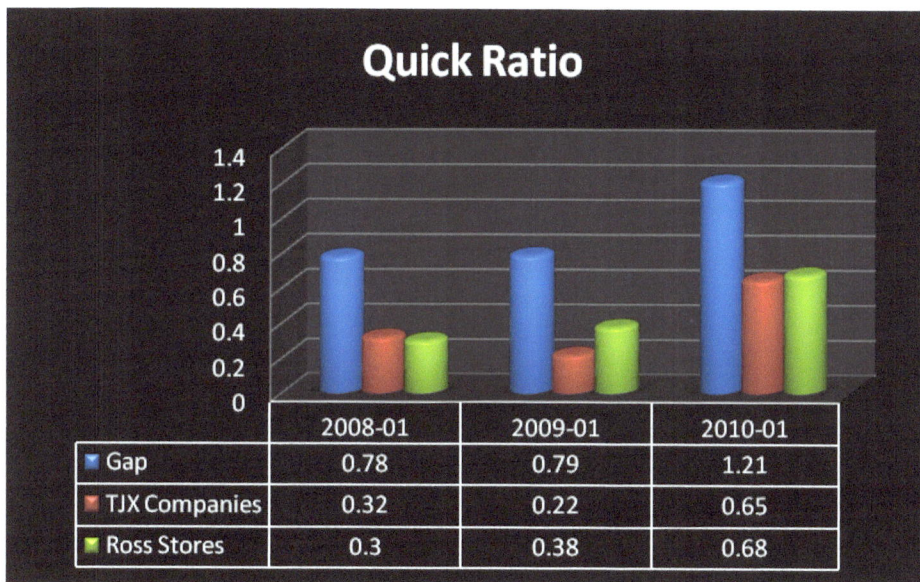

Quick Ratio	2008-01	2009-01	2010-01
Gap	0.78	0.79	1.21
TJX Companies	0.32	0.22	0.65
Ross Stores	0.3	0.38	0.68

Quick ratio is useful in determining the profitability of a company. It allows companies to decipher their abilities to meet their financial obligations with their quick or readily available assets. Liquid assets are the only ones that count in this test. Investors would like to see a quick ratio of at least 1:1 or 1.0. This means that the company has enough liquid assets that it would be able to pay off all its debts in a small amount of time if needed without liquefying any inventory quickly.

Out of all the companies, Gap Inc. shows the higher ratio within the FY of 2008 to FY 2010. Gap Inc.'s quick ratio is the only ratio that reached 1.0 and above compared to the top two competitors. The higher the ratio, the more profit the company is making in comparison to its debts. Gap is proving to be financially stable. In FY 2009, Ross Stores and TJX companies recovered a low quick ratio doubling the value in FY 2010. Despite the increase, they are still behind Gap, Inc and a lower quick ratio indicated impending financial disaster should the debts have to be repaid quickly.

Debt to Equity Ratio

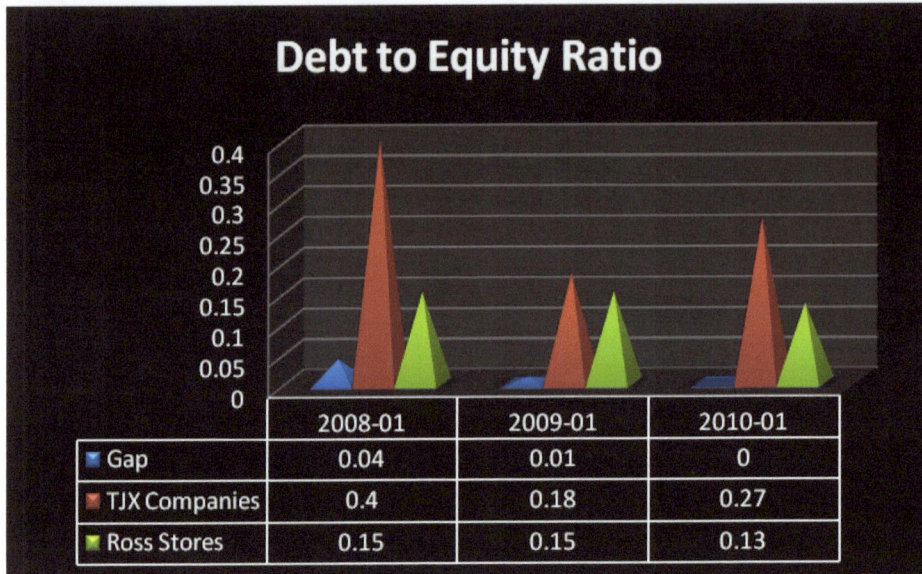

Debt to Equity Ratio

	2008-01	2009-01	2010-01
Gap	0.04	0.01	0
TJX Companies	0.4	0.18	0.27
Ross Stores	0.15	0.15	0.13

The debt-to-equity ratio is a measure of the relationship between the capital contributed by creditors and the capital contributed by shareholders. It also shows the extent to which shareholders' equity can fulfill a company's obligations to creditors in the event of liquidation. As illustrated above, all companies have maintained a low debt-to-equity ratio from FY 2008-FY 2010. As the years progress, all companies have been decreasing this ratio. However, Gap Inc. maintained the lowest debt-to-equity ratio among its competitors. A low debt to equity ratio indicates lower risk, because debt holders have fewer claims on the company's assets. The companies above have not been aggressive in financing growth with debt and therefore are avoiding volatile earnings.

Efficiency Ratios

Receivables Turnover Ratio

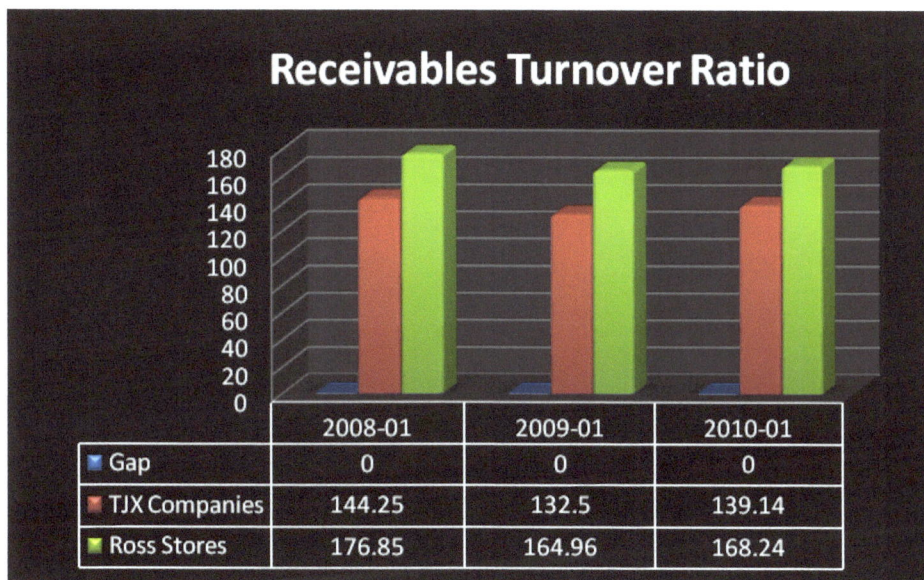

	2008-01	2009-01	2010-01
Gap	0	0	0
TJX Companies	144.25	132.5	139.14
Ross Stores	176.85	164.96	168.24

The receivable turnover ratio indicates the velocity of a company's debt collection, the number of times average receivables are turned over during a year. This ratio determines how quickly a company collects outstanding cash balances from its customers during an accounting period. It is an important indicator of a company's financial and operational performance and can be used to determine if a company is having difficulties collecting sales made on credit.

Gap, Inc indicates a low ratio for FY 2008 to FY 2010. The company should re-assess its credit policies in order to ensure the timely collection of imparted credit that is not earning interest for the firm. The lower the amount of uncollected monies from its operations, the higher this ratio will be. TJX Companies and Ross Stores demonstrate a high ratio. In contrast, if a company has more of its revenues awaiting receipt, the lower the ratio will be. The company's extension of credit and collection of accounts receivable is efficient.

Inventory Turnover Ratio

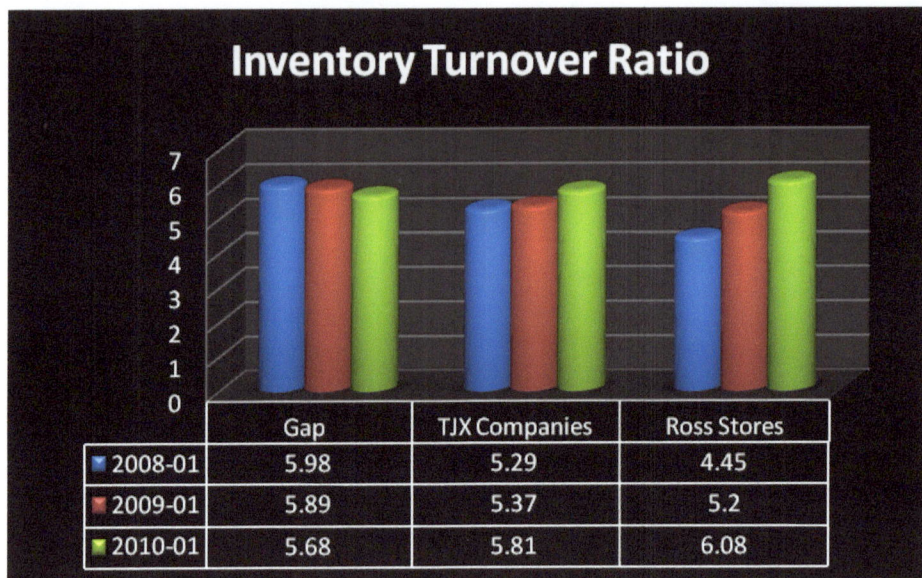

Inventory Turnover Ratio

	Gap	TJX Companies	Ross Stores
2008-01	5.98	5.29	4.45
2009-01	5.89	5.37	5.2
2010-01	5.68	5.81	6.08

The inventory turnover ratio is a common measure of the firm's operational efficiency in the management of its assets. Minimizing inventory holdings reduces overhead costs and, hence, improves the profitability performance of the enterprise. Inventory turnover is different for different industries. Businesses which trade in perishable goods have very higher turnover with comparison to those dealing in durables. A comparison would be fair only if made between businesses of same industry.

Gap, Inc Iventory turnover ratio has slowly been decreasing between FY 2008-2010 while their competitors have been increasing. To develop a high inventory turnover, The Gap must manage and sell its inventory efficiently. The faster the inventory sells the fewer funds the company has tied up. Companies have to be careful if they have a high inventory turnover as they are subject to stock outs. They should take advantage of additional resouces and large market share to create ore progressive supply chain mangment systems. Overall, the inventory turnover ratio is relatively similar to their competitors.

Asset Turnover Ratio

Asset Turnover	2008-01	2009-01	2010-01
Ross Stores	2.53	2.74	2.8
TJX Companies	2.94	2.97	2.97
Gap	1.92	1.89	1.83

The total asset turnover ratio measures the ability of a company to use its assets to efficiently generate sales. The lower the total asset turnover ratio, as compared to historical data for the firm and industry data, the more sluggish the firm's sales. Credit and collections policies have a significant impact on both sales and cash flow. A low ratio can indicate credit policies are lenient or that collection is inefficient while a high ratio might mean that credit policies are too strict and that sales are seeing a lost as a result.

Ross Stores and TJX Companies have been increasing their inventory turnover ratio for FY 2008-2010 unlike Gap, Inc where a decrease is illustrated above. The firm could be holding obsolete inventory and not selling inventory fast enough. With regard to accounts receivable, the firm's collection period could be too long and credit accounts may be on the books too long. Fixed assets, such as plant and equipment, could be sitting idle instead of being used to their full capacity. All of these issues could lower the total asset turnover ratio for Gap, Inc.

Profability Ratio

Gross Profit Margin

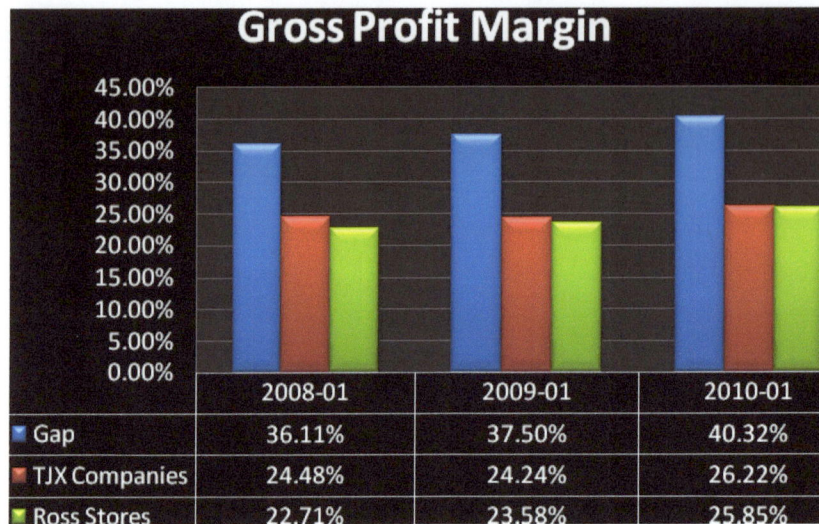

	2008-01	2009-01	2010-01
Gap	36.11%	37.50%	40.32%
TJX Companies	24.48%	24.24%	26.22%
Ross Stores	22.71%	23.58%	25.85%

This measure is used to assess a firm's financial health by revealing the proportion of revenues left over after accounting for the cost of goods sold. Gross profit margin serves as the source for paying additional expenses and future savings. Companies with low gross profit margins are susceptible to limited resources.

Gap, Inc. has the strongest gross profit margin which is vital to survival within the retail industry. Comparing TJX Companies and Ross Stores figures, they appear to be relativley close while increasing throughout the years. TJX Companies and Ross Stores both saw a slight decrease in FY 2009. A possible reason for this decline is due to the impact that rises in commodity prices which migh put difficulty on the aveage unit costs, manufacturing delays or unforseen deamnd that possiby impacted the gross margin. Unlike the competitors, The Gap have seen an increasing Gross Profit Margin over the last three years.

Operating Margin

Operating Margin

	2008-01	2009-01	2010-01
Ross Stores	7.05%	7.63%	10.11%
TJX Companies	6.66%	7.71%	9.62%
Gap	8.34%	10.66%	12.78%

Operating margin is a measurement of what proportion of a company's revenue is left over after paying for variable costs of production such as wages, raw materials, etc. A healthy operating margin is required for a company to be able to pay for its fixed costs, such as interest on debt. The higher the operating margin, the more profitable a company's core business is.

Gap, Inc. for the past three years has been increased by nearly 2% every year. When compared to the competitors, Gap is performing better than the average. TJX Companies have been increasing by 1% every year for the past three years while ROSS stores has had a minimal increase from FY 2008-2009 and nearly a 3% increase for 2010. Several things can affect operating margin such as pricing strategy, prices for raw materials, or labor costs, but because these items directly relate to the day-to-day decisions managers make, operating margin is also a measure of managerial flexibility and competency, particularly during tough economic times These strong companies have proven their stability when the economy took a downturn.

Pre-Tax Profit Margin

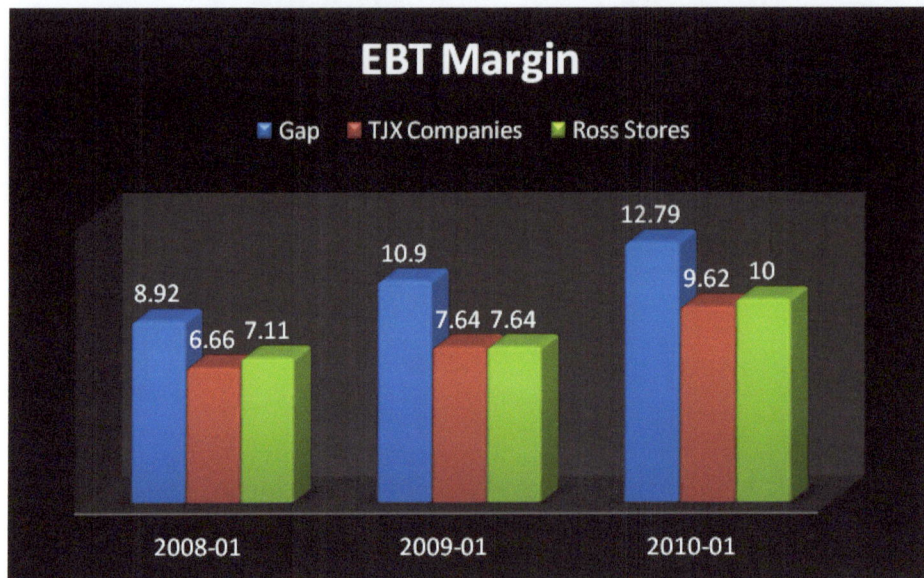

EBT margin shows company's earnings before tax as a percentage of net sales revenues. This ratio is very close to the net income margin as it also shows "bottom line" profit, except for the fact that the deducted income taxes are not excluded, and that's why this ratio is sometimes called pretax profit margin. Data to calculate this ratio is collected from the income statement. None of the three companies have a decreasing pretax profit margin. However, Gap seems to be increasing at a faster rate which means they have a strong hold on their business. If a decrease trend had appeared, it would have been important to monitor because it may have signaled a threat of a new entrant in the industry.

Net Profit Margin

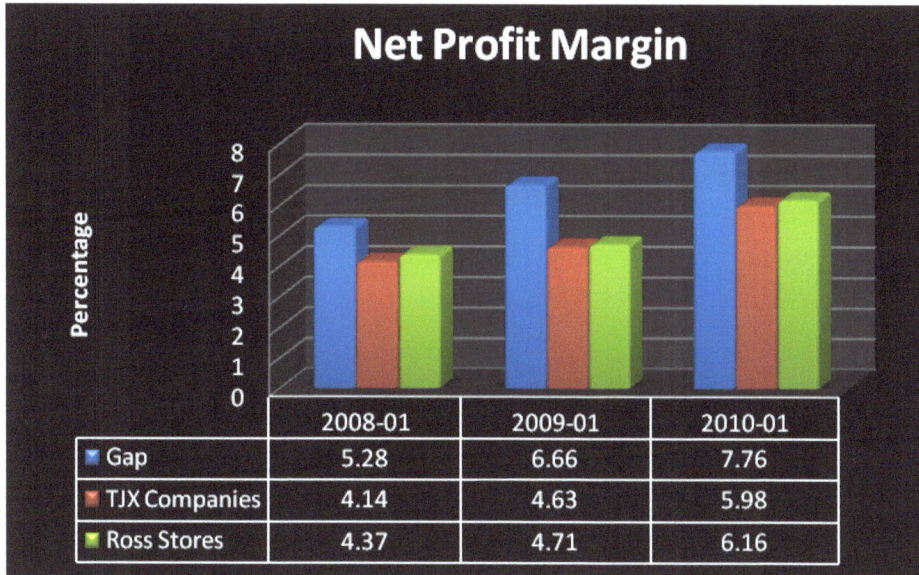

	2008-01	2009-01	2010-01
Gap	5.28	6.66	7.76
TJX Companies	4.14	4.63	5.98
Ross Stores	4.37	4.71	6.16

Net profit margin measures how much of each dollar earned by the company is translated into profits. It is mostly used to compare company's results over time and an indicator of how efficient a company is and how well it controls its costs. A low profit margin indicates a low margin of safety: higher risk that a decline in sales will erase profits and result in a net loss. The higher the margin is, the more effective the company is in converting revenue into actual profit. Net profit margin provides clues to the company's pricing policies, cost structure and production efficiency. Gap's numbers overall are higher and each company is demonstrating a positive increase FY 2008 to FY 2010.

Return On Assets

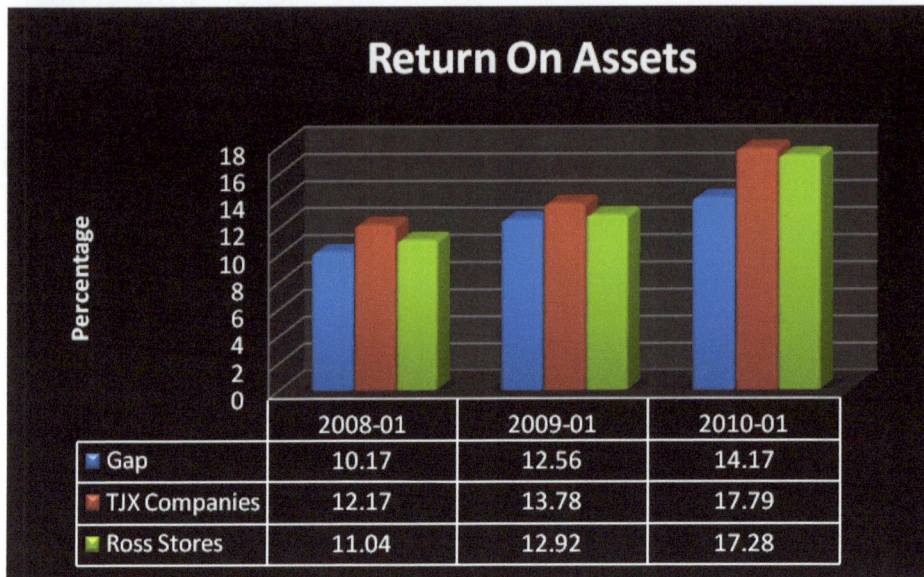

Return On Assets

	2008-01	2009-01	2010-01
Gap	10.17	12.56	14.17
TJX Companies	12.17	13.78	17.79
Ross Stores	11.04	12.92	17.28

This ratio indicates how profitable a company is relative to its total assets. It illustrates how well management is employing the company's total assets to make a profit. The higher the return, the more efficient management is in utilizing its assets base.

Return on assets indicates the number of cents earned on each dollar of assets. Thus higher values of return on assets show that business is more profitable. Unfortunately, The Gap has the lowest return on assets when compared to their major competitors. However, all three companies have been increasing their ROA which is an indication that the profitability of the company is improving. Conversely, a decreasing trend means that profitability is deteriorating. Both Ross Stores and TJX Companies saw a positive jump from FY 2009 to FY 2010.

Return On Equity

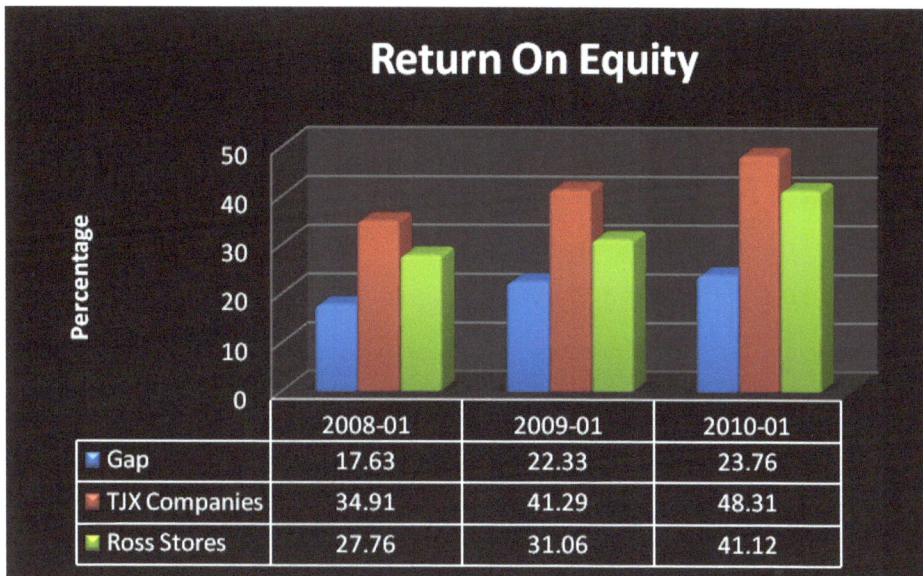

Return On Equity

	2008-01	2009-01	2010-01
Gap	17.63	22.33	23.76
TJX Companies	34.91	41.29	48.31
Ross Stores	27.76	31.06	41.12

One of the most important measurements is return on equity which reveals how much profit a company earned in comparison to the total amount of shareholder equity found on the balance sheet. A sustainable return on equity maximizes return on sales, asset turnover and financial leverage, and allows a sustainable growth rate to be achieved by optimizing these three indicators with the dividend payout ratio.

All three companies experience an increase in ROE during the past three years. However, Gap noticeable maintains the lowest return on equity out of the three firms which reflects negatively on the level of alignment to a strategic vision that is achieved by that company's board in its' decision-making, and implemented by its' leadership and ultimately delivered by its employees.

2. Altman

The Altman Z-Score helps investors to gauge the probability of a company going bankrupt.

There are 5 variables:

$X1$ = (Working Capital/Total Assets).

$X2$ = (Retained Earnings/Total Assets).

$X3$ = (EBITDA/Total Assets).

$X4$ = (Market Value of Equity/Total Liabilities).

$X5$ = (Net Sales/Total Assets).

$$Z = 1.2*X1 + 1.4*X2 + 3.3*X3 + 0.6*X4 + 1.0*X5.$$

The Interpretation of Altman Z-Score:

Z-SCORE ABOVE 3.0 – 'Safe' based on the financial figures only.

Z-SCORE BETWEEN 2.7 and 2.99 –'Exercise Caution'.

Z-SCORE BETWEEN 1.8 and 2.7 – Good chance of the company going bankrupt within 2 years of operations from the date of financial figures given.

Z-SCORE BELOW 1.80- Probability of financial catastrophe is high.

GAP VS THE TJX COMPANIES

Term:	Year End 28-Jan-12		Year End 29-Jan-11		Year End 30-Jan-10		Year End 31-Jan-09		Year End 02-Feb-08	
	GPS	TJX	GPS	TJX	GPS	TJX	GPS	TJX	GPS	TJX
Altman Z-Score	4.22	6.99	6.14	6.15	5.73	5.91	4.72	5.32	5.70	5.36

GAP VS ROSS STORES

Term:	Year End 28-Jan-12		Year End 29-Jan-11		Year End 30-Jan-10		Year End 31-Jan-09		Year End 02-Feb-08	
	GPS	ROST	GPS	ROST	GPS	ROST	GPS	ROST	GPS	ROST
Altman Z-Score	4.22	7.44	6.14	6.26	5.73	5.66	4.72	5.34	5.70	4.80

All three companies scored 3.0 and above which portrays to investors the companies are "safe" based on financial figures.

3. Tobin's Q

Market Value Per Share	Book Value Per Share	Tobin's Q's

GAP	34.9	6.59	5.295902883
TJX	43.54	4.65	9.36344086
Ross	55.32	7.77	7.11969112

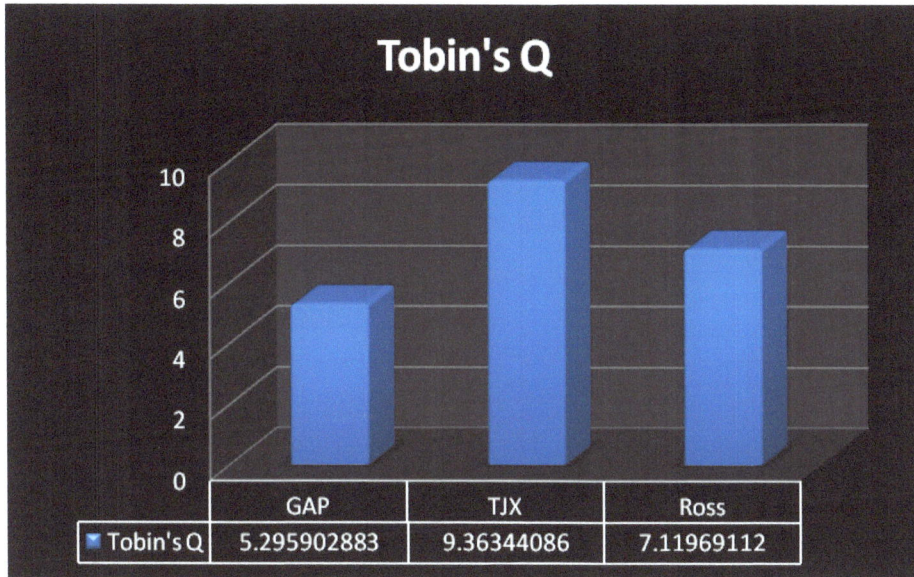

Tobin's Q

	GAP	TJX	Ross
Tobin's Q	5.295902883	9.36344086	7.11969112

4. DuPont Analysis

Gap, Inc. ($ in millions)

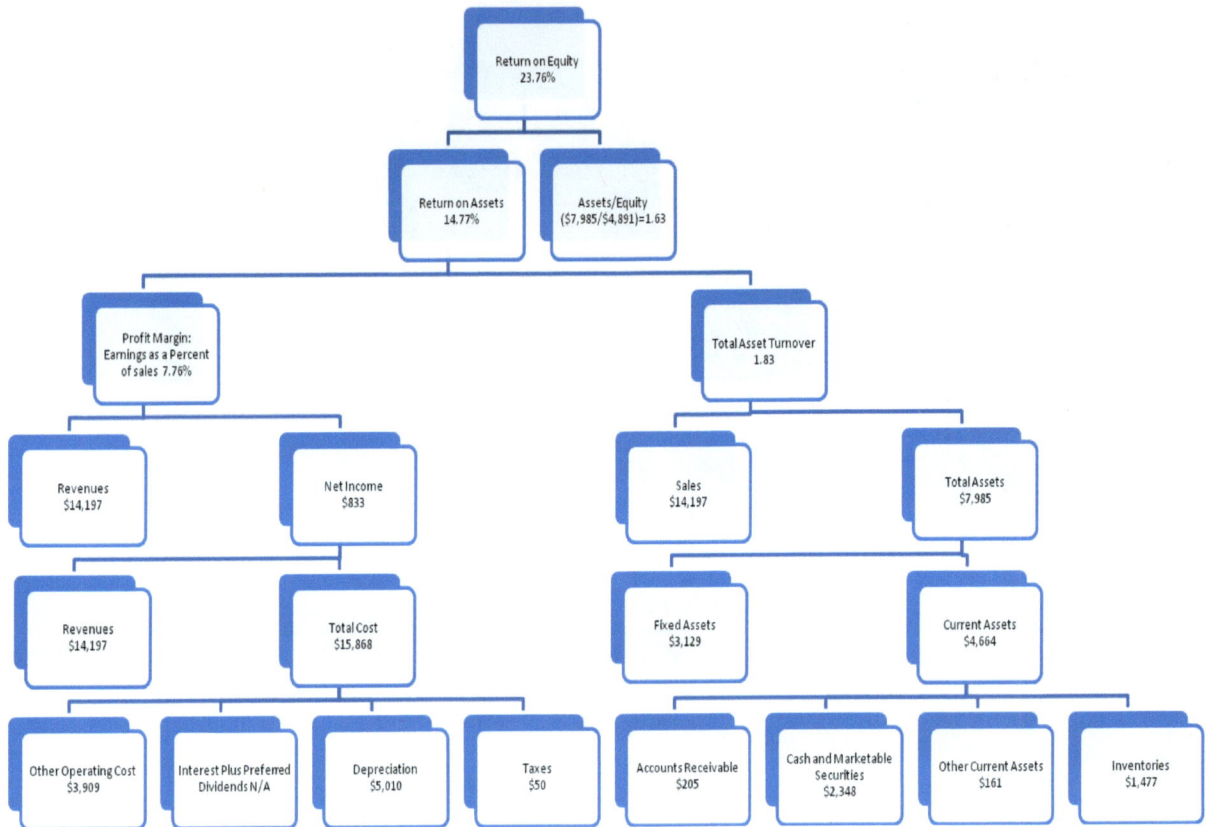

I. PESTEL Analysis

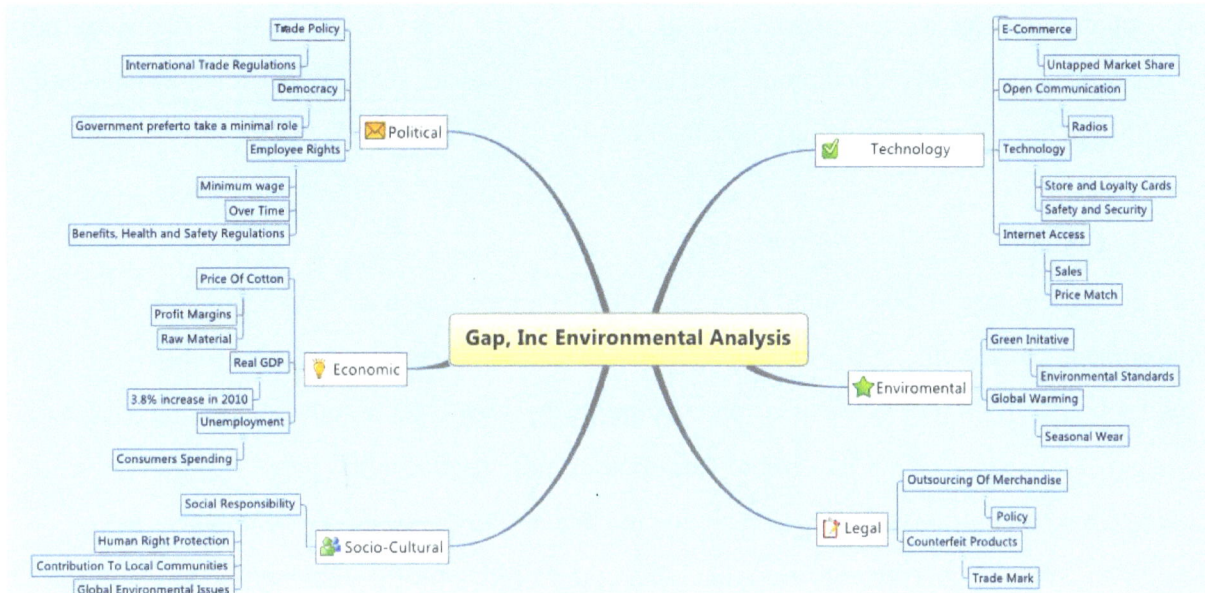

Gap, Inc Environmental Analysis mind map with branches: **Political** (Trade Policy, International Trade Regulations, Democracy, Government prefer to take a minimal role, Employee Rights); **Economic** (Minimum wage, Over Time, Benefits, Health and Safety Regulations, Price Of Cotton, Profit Margins, Raw Material, Real GDP, 3.8% increase in 2010, Unemployment, Consumers Spending); **Socio-Cultural** (Social Responsibility, Human Right Protection, Contribution To Local Communities, Global Environmental Issues); **Technology** (E-Commerce, Untapped Market Share, Open Communication, Radios, Technology, Store and Loyalty Cards, Safety and Security, Internet Access, Sales, Price Match); **Enviromental** (Green Initative, Environmental Standards, Global Warming, Seasonal Wear); **Legal** (Outsourcing Of Merchandise, Policy, Counterfeit Products, Trade Mark).

1. Political

Governments prefer to take a minimal role in the domestic economy. As a result, the U.S. has a small social safety net and business firms in the U.S. face less regulation than firms in many other nations. Employee rights in the United States have a substantial effect on business. With the apparel industry being labor-intensive, the effect employees laws have are significant. Employee laws to consider are minimum wage, over time, benefits and health and safety regulations. Overtime pay at a rate of not less than one and one-half times their regular rates of pay is required after 40 hours of work in a workweek. As well as minimum wage and over-time pay, employees are given the right to benefit plans. The ERISA, which is the Employee Retirement Income Security Act, sets uniform minimum standards to ensure that employee benefit plans are established and maintained in a fair and financially sound manner.

2. Economic

The world price of cotton represents a significant industry cost. As the price of cotton rises, so does the price of clothing. Higher clothing prices mean higher purchasing costs and falling profit margins for family clothing stores. This driver is expected to decline during 2012. Real GDP is the total value of a country's production, adjusted for inflation. The US real GDP increased in 2010 by 3.8% following a 1.7% decrease in 2009. The rise in GDP growth tells investors that as the economy grows, the U.S. apparel retail industry will experience growth as well. Retailers have cut employment at an annualized rate of 1.0% over the five-year period to 2012. With decreased sales volumes and climbing rent and advertising costs, industry participants have had to limit spending on expense items they can control.

3. Socio-Cultural

With the increasing globalization of business, society has also been more concern with the environment and benefits of the employees. The society demands social responsibility which includes human right protection of corporate employees, contribution to local communities and environmental changes. Gap Inc. employees number more than 134,000 people around the world and the company culture encourages each one to "Wear your passion." The company also focuses on choosing investments that can create opportunities for the underserved youth in the developed world. For example, Gap has teamed up with Apparel Lesotho Alliance to Fight HIV/AIDS (ALAFA). For the past couple of years, Gap has sold a line of clothing to promote the RED Campaign. For each article of clothing sold, a portion of the profit is donated to the ALAFA foundation. The clothing is intentionally made in textile facilities in areas of Africa that are severely affected by AIDS, thus helping their local economies. Also, Gap Inc. believes environmental responsibility means far more than being "green" or selling green products. To have the greatest positive impact, Gap, Inc. focuses on the facilities operated because they can control the energy utilized and the waste created.

4. Technological

Modern technology has meant that retailers can now enhance the experience their customers receive more than ever before. Store and loyalty cards are one such use of technology as they not only reward shoppers with discounts and money off advantages but they also track spending habits and buying trends of their customers. Another new way in which forward thinking retailers are embracing technology to enhance their stores safety, security and communication is through the use of Two Way Radios. These provide retailers a way improve their communication and performance. Moreover, E-commerce is an untapped market and internet access implies new avenue for direct sales. The company's online presence is not only beneficial to the consumers but also to Gap because they are also able to enjoy low operational costs. Consumers are able to shop all Gap brands (Gap, Banana Republic, Old Navy and Piperlime) at the same time and ship all products for a flat rate of $7.

6. Environmental

Gap has completed a comprehensive inventory of its impact on global warming, and that the company expects to continue and extend its review in the future. Gap has established clear goals to reduce the company's energy use, and the company has reduced its impact on global warming (i.e. its greenhouse gas emissions or climate footprint). The company has also worked to foster climate awareness among consumers, employees, and other businesses. Gap has made public information available on its efforts to address global warming.

7. Legal

Estimated counterfeit sales of around $500 billion per year are a major problem for companies within the apparel and accessories markets. Gap suffers a minimum loss of $200 billion in revenue. In Europe, counterfeit products are estimated to be worth $8.2 billion. The availability of counterfeit products continues to erode market share and reduces the brand image.

J. SWOT Analysis

Strengths	Weaknesses
• Global presence catalyzed by franchise and company-owned stores and online presence • Well balanced portfolio of value as well as upscale brands • Strong margins compared to competitors	• Dependence on outside merchandise vendors for supply of products • Low productivity of company's stores
Opportunities	Threats
• Expanding presence in key growth markets • Growing market for plus size apparel for women in the US and the UK • Positive trends in the online channel	• Weak consumer spending in Europe and the US • High input cost can pressurize Gap Inc.'s margins • Growing market for counterfeit products

Strengths

- Global presence catalyzed by franchise and company-owned stores and online presence
    - Gap Inc. is gaining increased global market share through its multiple distribution channels (franchise and company-owned retail locations and online store)
- Well balanced portfolio of value as well as upscale brands
    - Gap Inc. connects with many target markets, as it offers brands for value customers through its Old Navy brand and high end customers through its Banana Republic brand
- Strong margins compared to competitors
    - Allows Gap Inc. to combat price competition while allowing the company to adjust for fluctuating cotton costs without passing the cost onto its customer through increased prices

Weaknesses

- Dependence on outside merchandise vendors for supply of products
    - With heavy dependence on outside vendors to supply Gap Inc. products, all cost associated with the supplier channel is passed onto Gap Inc. and increases cost of goods sold and decreases margins
- Low productivity of company's stores
    - Gap is closing many retail locations globally due to decreasing revenue per employee figures, in hopes to decrease costs and maintain employees with the highest productivity

Opportunities

- Expanding presence in key growth markets
    - Increasing international growth
- Growing market for plus size apparel for women in the US and the UK
    - Increasing obesity problems for women in the US and the UK create an increasing demand for clothing in the women's plus size industry
- Positive trends in the online channel
    - While overall customer spending is decreasing, consumers are increasing spending through online channels

Threats

- Weak consumer spending in Europe and the US
    - o Due to economic downturns in Europe and the US, consumer spending has decreased
- High input cost can pressurize Gap Inc.'s margins
    - o An increased input cost to produce cotton (seeding and specialized equipment) is leading to decreasing crop yields, therefore increasing the overall cost of cotton in the commodity marketplace. Gap Inc. is realizing increased cost of goods sold and decreasing overall margins
- Growing market for counterfeit products
    - o The market for counterfeit products is increasing, therefore providing consumers with less expensive alternatives to Gap Inc. brands

TOWS Matrix for GAP Inc.	External Opportunities (O) 1. Focus on E-Commerce 2. Emerging Markets 3. 4.	External Threats (T) 1. Emerging fast fashion retail 2. Consumer Preferences 3. Currency Fluctuation 4.
Internal Strengths (S) 1. Global Presence 2. Well Balanced 3. Strong Margins 4. Online Value	-Offer Plus Size Clothing in Banana Republic and GAP INC. -Free Online Shipping -Incorporate Online ordering to Brick and Mortar Shipping Maxi-Maxi Strategy	-Reduce the Cost of Goods Sold and Overhead, this will increase the profit margin. -Create Brick and Mortar Stores for Piperlime and Athleta -Create marketing campaign that emphasizes the quality of GAP products -Streamline logistics and distribution centers. Maxi-Mini Strategy
Internal Weaknesses (W) 1. Outsider Rely 2. Outside Vendors 3. Low Productivity 4. Diversification	-Build new stores in emerging markets. -Enforce copyright infringement -Promote Online Sales, which incorporates Athleta and Piperlime. -Create backward integration by purchasing textile mills. Mini-Maxi Strategy	-Get rid of low producing stores. -Bring High End names to incorporate into main stream products. These can be multi-layered in quality. -Negotiate better contracts with current vendors or find new vendors. Mini-Mini Strategy

K. Market Share Data Graphs

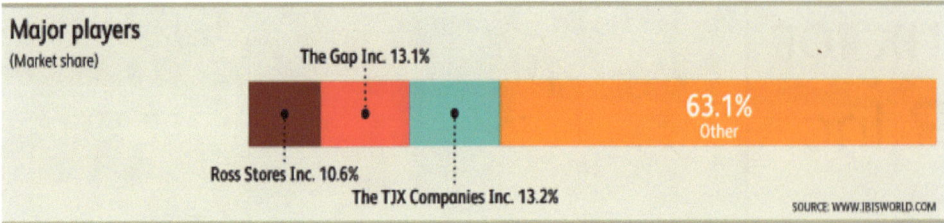

Major players
(Market share)

The Gap Inc. 13.1%

63.1%
Other

Ross Stores Inc. 10.6%

The TJX Companies Inc. 13.2%

SOURCE: WWW.IBISWORLD.COM

The chart shows the market share of each major player and the collective concentration of all dominant industry players. There is room for Gap, Inc. to grow and obtain a larger market share.

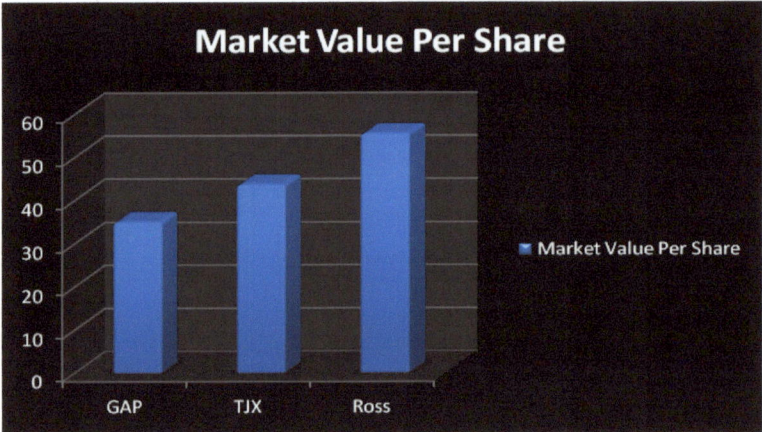

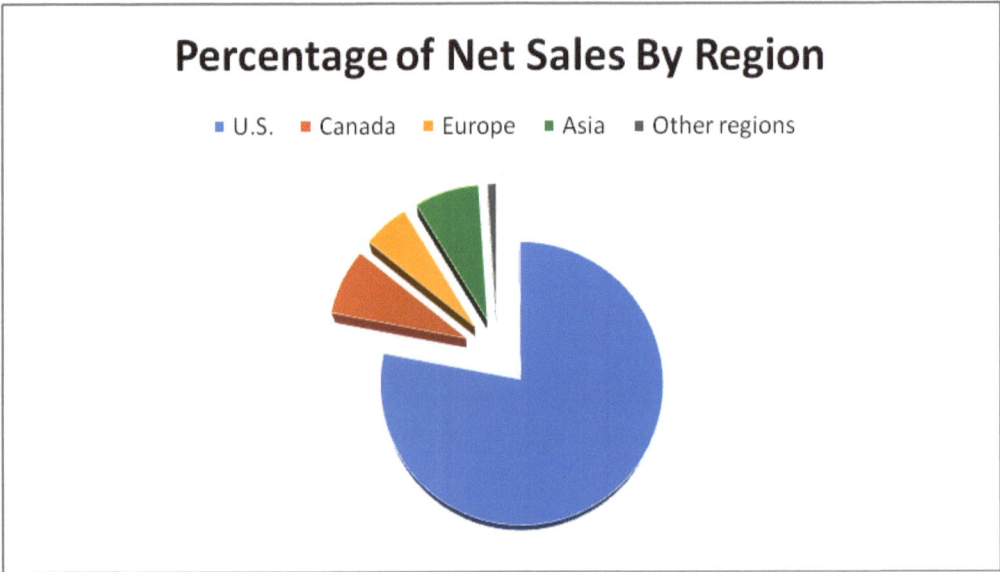

Market Value Per Share

60
50
40
30
20
10
0

GAP   TJX   Ross

■ Market Value Per Share

Percentage of Net Sales By Region

■ U.S.   ■ Canada   ■ Europe   ■ Asia   ■ Other regions

The chart above illustrates that 71% of Gap, Inc.'s net sales are retained from the US region. The remaining regions have a percentage that are relativley similar. Canada and Asia both contribute7%, Europe contributes 5% and the other regions accumulated contribute 1%.

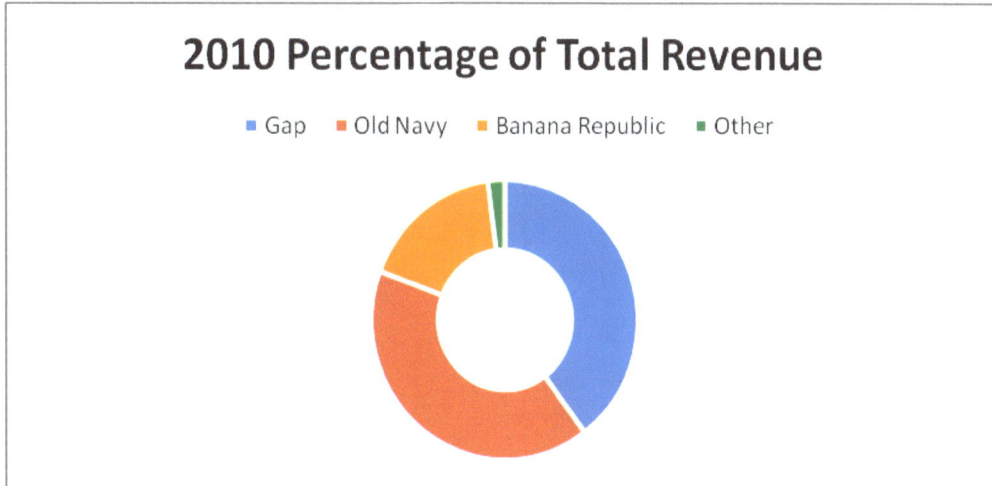

2010 Percentage of Total Revenue

■ Gap ■ Old Navy ■ Banana Republic ■ Other

For the fiscal year of 2010, The Gap obtained the uppermost revenue compared to their other divisions. Old Navy obtains the next highest revenue while Banana Republic and the others retained a less significant amount.

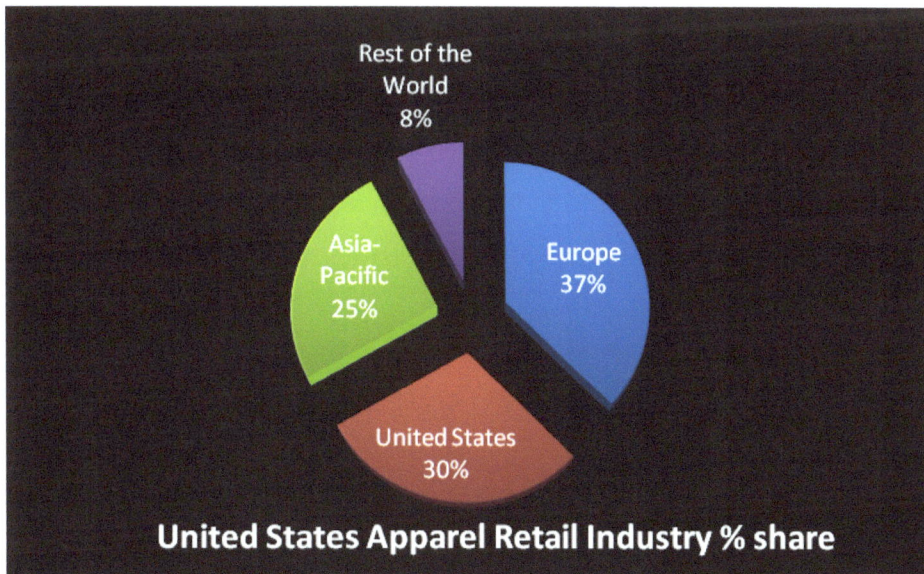

Rest of the World 8%

Asia-Pacific 25%

Europe 37%

United States 30%

United States Apparel Retail Industry % share

IBIS World forecasts that concentration will remain relatively steady over the five years to 2017 as consumers regain their purchasing power and switch from off-price retailers like TJX and Ross to higher-priced, higher-quality brands like the Gap's Banana Republic segment.

The United States accounts for 29.6% of the global apparel retail industry value. Europe accounts for a further 37.3% of the global industry which indicates that Gap, Inc should take into account the possibility for further growth within the European Countries. Asia-Pacific accounts a 25.5% share while the rest of the world obtains a smaller share of 7.7%.

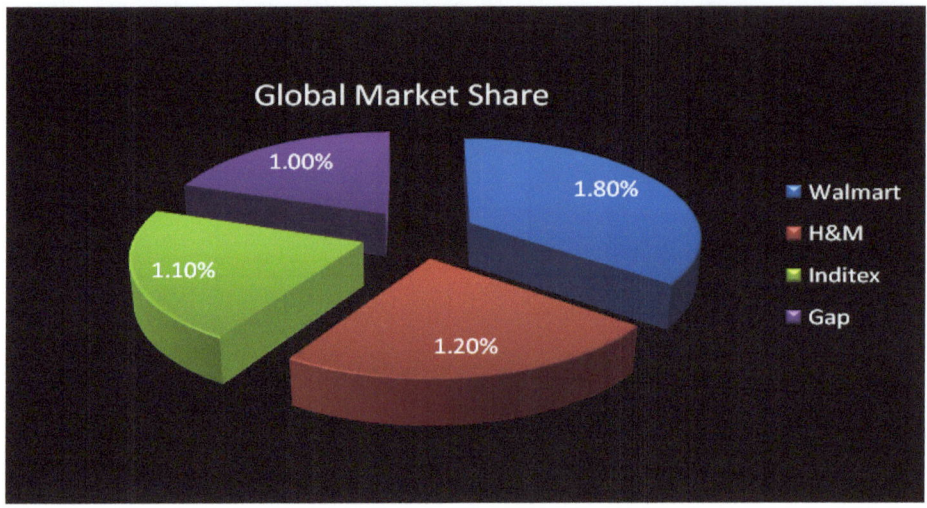

The top four industry participants within the domestic market share include the TJX Companies, The Gap, Ross Stores and Abercrombie & Fitch. However, within the global industry, the top four industry participants include Wal-mart, H&M, Inditex and Gap. Wal-mart is the leading player in the global apparel, accessories and luxury good market, generating a 1.8 share of the markets value. H&M, Inditex and Gap are account for a relatively smaller portion of the market.

II. *FOCAL POINTS FOR ACTION*

A. Short Term Goal

1. Increase short-term profits

Gap, the United State's largest clothing chain, is planning to close one-fifth of its stores in the United States by 2013. Gap detailed plans to close 189 locations, 21 % of its stores, in n attempt to increase short-term profits while gearing up for plans to expand overseas. This announcement is in line with the company's goals of reducing the square footage in United States stores by 10% while doubling revenue from outside the United States to 30% by 2013."The combination of our global strategy and formidable growth platform puts us in a strong position to expand our reach into the top 10 apparel markets worldwide," said Gap CEO Glenn. "With a strong management team in place, we're well positioned for sustained growth across the business."

2. Triple Stores In China within one year

The corporation, which runs the Gap, Old Navy and Banana Republic, and Piperlime, is looking overseas for more revenue as American consumers continue to spend less due to the country's economic woes. Gap plans to triple the number of Gap stores in China from the 15 currently in place to about 45 by the end of 2012. The reduction in stores in the United States will leave about 700 Gap namesake locations in the country by the end of 2013, down from the 1056 locations in 2007.

B. Long Term Goal

1. Successfully compete within a highly competitive retail industry.

We compete with local, national, and global department stores, specialty and discount store chains, independent retail stores, and online businesses that market similar lines of merchandise. Our long term goals in order to face to variety of competitive challenges include:

- Anticipating and quickly responding to changing fashion trends and consumer demands
- Attracting consumer traffic
- Competitively pricing our products and achieving customer perception of value

- Maintain favorable brand recognition and effectively marketing our products to consumers in several diverse market segments
- Developing innovative, high quality products in sizes, colors, and styles that appeal to consumers of varying age groups and tastes
- Sourcing merchandise efficiently
- Providing strong and effective marketing support.

2. International Expansion

Our current strategies include international expansion in a number of countries around the world through a number of channels and brands, including franchise. For example, we currently plan to open Old Navy stores outside of North America, open additional Gap stores in China, open additional international outlet stores, and continue to grow online sales internationally. We have limited experience operating in some of these locations. In many of these locations, we face major, established competitors. In addition, in many of these locations, the real estate, employment and labor, transportation and logistics, regulatory, and other operating requirements differ dramatically from those in the places where we have experience. However, we believe our marketing strategies and our brand value will help us succeed globally.

3. Expand our franchise business

Enter into franchise agreements with unaffiliated franchisees to operate stores in many countries around the world. Under these agreements, third parties operate, or will operate, stores that sell apparel and related products under our brand names. The effect of these arrangements on our business and results of operations is uncertain and will depend upon various factors, including the demand for our products in new markets internationally and our ability to successfully identify appropriate third parties to act as franchisees, distributors, or in a similar capacity. In addition, certain aspects of these arrangements are not directly within our control, such as the ability of these third parties to meet their projections regarding store locations, store openings, and sales. Other risks that may affect these third parties include general economic conditions in specific countries or markets, foreign exchange, changes in diplomatic and trade relationships, and political instability. Moreover, while the agreements we have entered into and plan to enter into in future provide us with certain termination rights, the value of our brands will be protected since these third parties are obligated to their stores in a manner consistent with our requirements regarding our brand identities and customer experience standards.

Our success is largely dependent upon our ability to gauge the tastes of our customers and to provide merchandise that satisfies customer demand in a timely manner. However, lead times for many of our purchases are long, which may make it more difficult for us to respond rapidly to new or changing fashion trends or consumer acceptance of our products. The global specialty retail business fluctuates according to changes in consumer preferences, dictated in part by fashion and season. To the extent we misjudge the market for our merchandise or the products suitable for local markets or fail to execute trends and deliver product to market as timely as our competitors, our sales will be adversely affected, and the markdowns required to move the resulting excess inventory will adversely affect our operating results. Some of our past product offerings have not been well received by our broad and diverse customer base. Merchandise misjudgments could have a material adverse effect on our operating results.

Our ability to anticipate and effectively respond to changing fashion trends depends in part on our ability to attract and retain key personnel in our design, merchandising, marketing, and other functions. Competition for this personnel is intense, and we cannot be sure that we will be able to attract and retain a sufficient number of qualified personnel in future periods.
Fluctuations in the global specialty retail business especially affect the inventory owned by apparel retailers, as merchandise usually must be ordered well in advance of the season and frequently before fashion trends are evidenced by customer purchases. In addition, the nature of the global specialty retail business requires us to carry a significant amount of inventory, especially prior to the peak holiday selling season when we build up our inventory levels. We must enter into contracts for the purchase and manufacture of merchandise well in advance of the applicable selling season. As a result, we are vulnerable to demand and pricing shifts and to suboptimal selection and timing of merchandise purchases. In the past, we have not always predicted our customers' preferences and acceptance levels of our fashion items with accuracy. If

sales do not meet expectations, too much inventory may cause excessive markdowns, and therefore, lower than planned margins.

Independent third parties manufacture nearly all of our products for us. As a result, we are directly impacted by increases in the cost of those products. For example, cotton prices rose substantially during fiscal 2011, which put significant pressure on our average unit costs and gross margins. If we experience significant increases in demand or need to replace an existing vendor, there can be no assurance that additional manufacturing capacity will be available when required on terms that are acceptable to us or that any vendor would allocate sufficient capacity to us in order to meet our requirements. In addition, for any new manufacturing source, we may encounter delays in production and added costs as a result of the time it takes to train our vendors in our methods, products, quality control standards, and environmental, labor, health, and safety standards. Moreover, in the event of a significant disruption in the supply of the fabrics or raw materials used by our vendors in the manufacture of our products, our vendors might not be able to locate alternative suppliers of materials of comparable quality at an acceptable price. Any delays, interruption, or increased costs in the manufacture of our products could result in lower sales and net income.

Independent vendors manufacture nearly all of our products outside of our principal sales markets, third parties must transport our products over large geographic distances. Delays in the shipment or delivery of our products due to the availability of transportation, work stoppages, port strikes, infrastructure congestion, or other factors, and costs and delays associated with transitioning between vendors, could adversely impact our financial performance. Manufacturing delays or unexpected demand for our products may require us to use faster, but more expensive, transportation methods such as aircraft, which could adversely affect our gross margins. In addition, the cost of fuel is a significant component in transportation costs, so increases in the price of petroleum products can adversely affect our gross margins.

III. DEVELOP ALTERNATIVES:

A. Boston Consulting Group Matrix

The following represents an estimate of where Gap division companies are using the Boston Consulting Group (BCG) matrix.

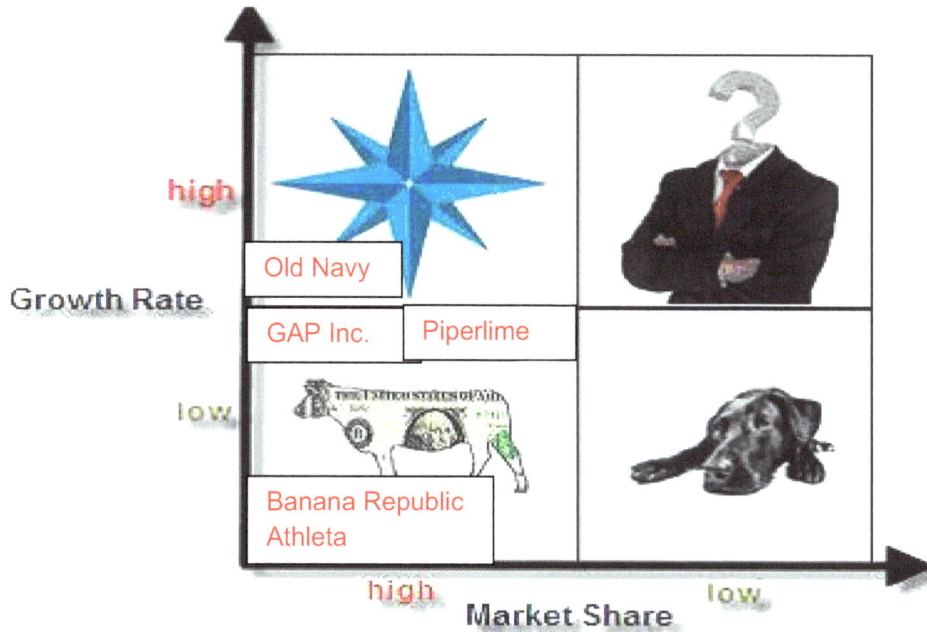

B.   Competitive Position

Gap uses Cost Leadership. Gap uses key marketing like "Love comes in every shade" and
"Powers to the She"

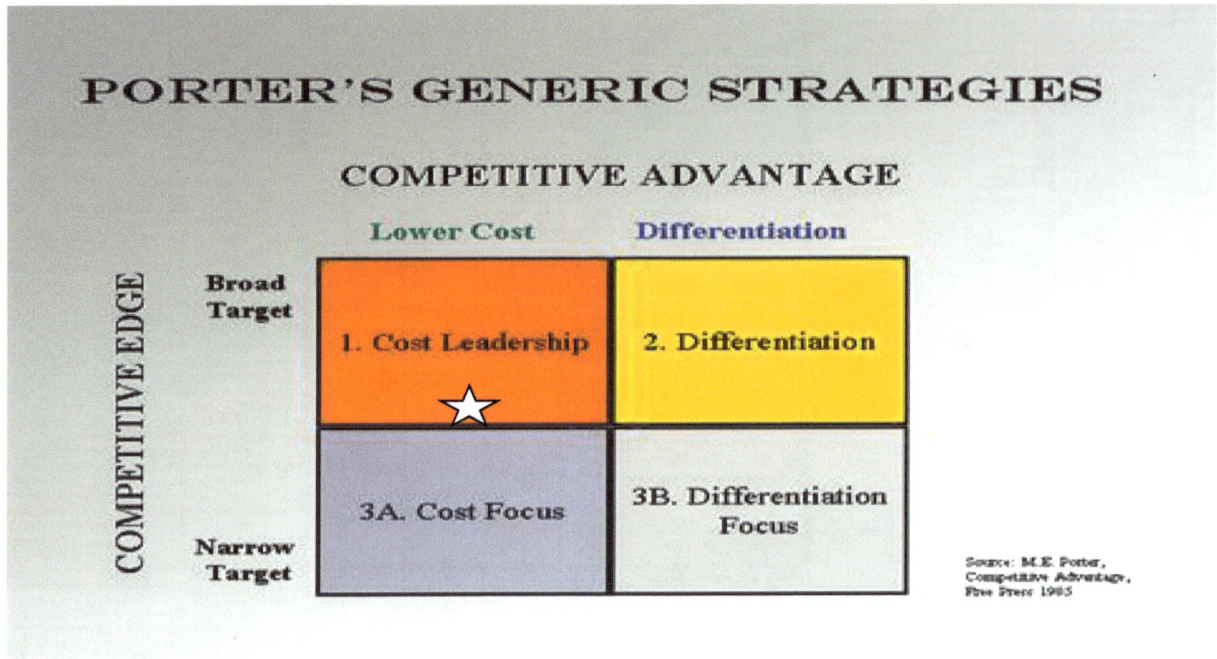

PORTER'S GENERIC STRATEGIES

COMPETITIVE ADVANTAGE

		Lower Cost	Differentiation
COMPETITIVE EDGE	**Broad Target**	1. Cost Leadership ★	2. Differentiation
	Narrow Target	3A. Cost Focus	3B. Differentiation Focus

Source: M.E. Porter,
Competitive Advantage,
Free Press 1985

Gap and Low Cost Leadership: Gap Inc. owns various stores and is best at low cost and product
differentiation. Since Gap Inc. owns a variety of their higher end stores such as Banana Republic
and Gap followed by a more cost effective alternative like Old Navy. This industry is highly
competitive so Gap Inc. must focus on low cost, trendy and buzz worthy clothing. Gap Inc. has
performed well in this endeavor.

C. Competitive Strategy Options

Strategic Issues

1. **Enhancing the Shopping Experience:**
   - To survive they must enhance the shopping experience for the consumers.
   - GAP Inc. must ensure that they are ever evolving and leveraging social media and new technologies available.
   - The experience must be visually pleasing.
   - Customers must feel that the shopping is trendy and hip.
   - Large Market Shares creates a lack of effectiveness and efficiency of resources.
   - **With such a revolution of social media why not incorporate it in the shopping experience?**

2. **Enhancing the Brand:**
   - Brand name associated with poor quality and high cost.
   - No trendy logo that creates brand loyalty or boutique following
   - Archaic use of marketing that lacks inspiration
   - The brand does not synchronize or energize behind a line.
   - **How can a brand name expect to survive with such a diversified market share?**

3. **Enhancing Global Recognition**
   - In order to achieve growth GAP INC. must focus on expansion in BRICS countries while being a low cost leader.
   - It is important that GAP INC. become synonymous with high quality and.
   - Using multi-pronged social media that focused on the social media methods within that country.

With GAP INC. having efficiency's and a good market share, why not continue to expand in the BRICS countries?

D. Rumelt's criteria

Rumelt's Criteria GAP Inc.

Strategy	Consistency	Consonance	Feasibility	Advantage	Total
Market Penetrations					
Gaining competitors customers	5	4	4	4	17
Increasing Advertising	5	5	4	4	18
Market Development					
Global Expansion	4	3	3	4	14
Reaching into New Market Segments					
Shoes	5	5	4	4	18
Watches	4	3	3	5	15
Scents	3	4	4	3	14
Product Development					
Business Attire	5	4	4	4	17
Sports Wear	5	4	3	3	15
High Quality Clothing	5	5	4	4	18
Night Wear	3	3	4	3	13
Shoes	4	4	3	3	14
Watches	3	3	3	3	12
Plus Size Clothing	5	4	4	4	17
Middle Aged Clothing	5	3	3	4	15
Concentric Diversification					
Purchase Eddie Bauer	3	3	4	3	13
Purchase Guess	3	4	4	4	15
Purchase Land's End	4	4	4	4	16
New Shoe Division	3	3	4	3	13
New Watch Division	3	2	3	2	10
New Scent Division	3	4	5	4	16
Horizontal Integration					
Acquire Aeropostale	4	4	4	3	15

Acquire Buckle	4	3	3	3	13
Acquire Hollister	4	4	4	4	16
Acquire Forever 21	3	3	3	4	13
Backward Vertical Integration					
Acquire Textile Plant	4	4	5	5	18
Acquire Clothing Manufacturing	4	5	5	5	19
Acquire Scent Manufacturing	3	3	3	3	12
Acquire Apparel Manufacturing	3	4	4	4	15
Forward Vertical Integration					
Purchase Credit Card Services	1	2	3	3	9
Purchase Online Market Seller	1	3	1	4	9
Purchase Jewelry Stores	2	2	2	2	8
Divestiture					
Sell Outlet Stores	1	2	1	1	5
Sell Athleta	1	1	3	3	8
Sell Piperlime	1	1	3	3	8

E.   Porter's Five Forces

Buyer Power	
Degree of Rivalry	 The degree of rivalry for GAP Inc is relatively high. GAP faces various competitors throughout the U.S. and increasingly across the globe as they seek to expand. TJX companies and Ross Stores are the main competitors, but the clothing industry has many competitors of various sizes that pose an impact on GAP Inc. GAP is trying to diversify the product line and establish a strong presence of consumer loyalty.

Substitutes	**Threat of substitutes** 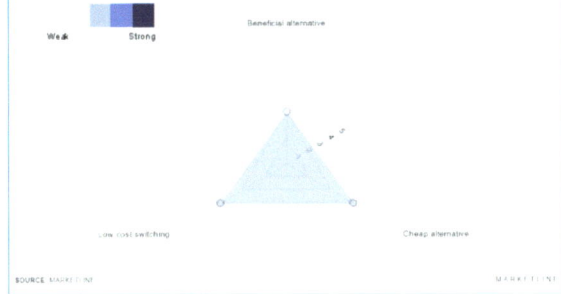 Figure 9: Factors influencing the threat of substitutes in the global apparel & non-apparel manufacturing market, 2011
New Entrants	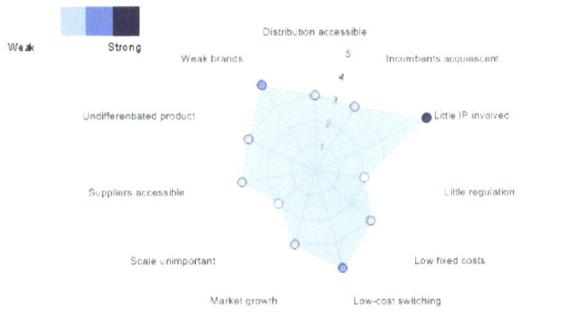
Supplier Power	

III. DECISIONS AND RECOMMENDATIONS

A. *Corporate*

"Gap Inc. was founded on the principle of doing business responsibly, honestly and ethically. We take corporate compliance very seriously. Our comprehensive corporate compliance program is designed to ensure that all employees and the company's Board of Directors (directors) not only meet legal requirements around the world, but also operate responsibly and with integrity in everything they do.

We listen to our customers around the world, and share their expectations. For us, that means looking deeper into our supply chain to ensure that we take a responsible path throughout the product lifecycle,

As we continue to expand our presence internationally, we're more aware than ever how our decisions affect the communities in which we do business. And our philosophy is simple: We seek to make a positive, lasting impact on the people and in the places where we operate from the source to our stores." Gapinc.com

Objectives

- Increase international presence in major growth markets (Market Penetration)
- Invest heavily in international franchise expansion (Market Penetration)
- Increase sales by 2% annually over the next three years
- Diversify product lines across the Gap Inc. brand (Product Development)
- Continue to develop and diversify online presence and customer experience (Market Development)
- Increase Return on Equity from 23.7% to 27% over the next three years
- Strive to remain the industry leader
- Acquire major textile supplier

Strategies

- Increase the number of international brick and mortar locations by 10% over the next three years
- Appoint a head of International relations to oversee all international expansion

- Create an international headquarters in London, England
- Increase spending into R&D and product development initiatives
- Acquire new businesses with diversified product lines
- Purchasing local cotton producers in close proximity to growth market where store expansion is taking place

B. *Business*

Objectives
- Increase international Gap store presence by 3.5% over the next three years
- Expand Athleta brick and mortar stores into major U.S. markets
- Increase international Old Navy store presence by 3.5% over the next three years
- Increase Gap Outlet brick and mortar locations in Europe
- Expand Piperlime brand into mainstream brick and mortar retail locations

Strategies
- Open Gap franchise stores open in Kazakhstan, Serbia, Ukraine, Poland, Chile, Vietnam, Egypt and Morocco
- Open Gap store on China's largest e-commerce mall, Taobao
- Expand Athleta brand with brick and mortar store openings in major U.S. markets including New York, Los Angeles, Philadelphia and Minneapolis
- Open Banana Republic its first flagship store in Paris, France, on Avenue des Champs Élysées
- Open first Gap Outlet stores in China
- 45 Gap stores are slated to be open in China by the end of FY2012
- Open first Old Navy outside North America in Tokyo, Japan
- Open Gap franchise stores in Guam, Panama, South Africa, Georgia, Lebanon, Colombia, Azerbaijan, and Uruguay
- Addition of 20 Athleta stores to be opened in major U.S. markets by FY2012
- Test market a physical Piperlime store open in North America
- Make Gap and Banana Republic available online in Japan

C. *Functional*

Objectives

- Maintain inventory ratios through international expansion period
- Implement incentive programs to drive day to day employee performance
- Develop incentive program for online customer feedback
- Cut costs due to increased efficiency in the international distribution model

Strategies

- Develop effective inventory control systems which make transportation between international countries more efficient
- Evaluate trade laws in countries where suppliers are located and new franchises are built to make for cost reduction in the distribution chain
- Open first Gap Outlet stores in China
- Make Gap and Banana Republic available online in Japan

IV.   IMPLEMENTATION

Goal #1: Our main goal for the next three years, as outlined in the Decisions and Recommendations section, is to drastically increase our international brand presence. (Market Penetration)

Participants: Participants: Executive Leadership including CEO, President of Gap Inc., Senior Vice President of Global Real Estate and additionally the Retail Development team, Human Resource Management, and Global Marketing professionals.

Steps:

Appoint a head of International Relations to oversee all international expansion.

We will gain organization wide commitment through the development of an International Headquarters located in London, England. This will allow our international business units and their employees a much needed resource to help in their penetration of the foreign markets.

> Brick and mortar franchise locations
>
> Online presence and sales

Reorganizing the international corporate structure to include a head of International Relations and an international headquarters, will allow for a smooth transition leading into a major international expansion.

More extensive international expansion allows for better alignment with the inventory needs of the business, as store locations will be in closer proximity to the supply chain.

The leadership of the company is driving the expansion initiative and will be a major player in the hiring of the new head of International Relations, which will have a great impact on the daily operations of the business.

Fair compensation stemming from increasing sales due to expansion, will leave all members of the Gap team driving toward the same goal at an appropriate rate.

There will be many unforeseen challenges to overcome when entering new markets. Leadership has put plans in place to minimize the effect these challenges might have on the company and its employees.

With new international corporate restructuring, employees will have timely notification of decisions and changes as they are made or put into action. All communication will come from top down and filter through the proper management channels, where employees can ask questions or pose concerns during this time.

Goal #2: Development of Athleta and Piperlime brick and mortar locations in the United States over the next three years

Participants: CEO, President of Gap Inc., Senior Vice President of Global Real Estate, Retail Development team, Human Resource Management

Steps:

Executive leadership in partnership with the Retail Development and Real Estate team will need to determine the best locations for the launch of these online brands into the brick and mortar retail market.

Due to Gap's history and experience in retail, the addition of these stores should be aligned with the current supply, human resource and logistical strategies of its current brick and mortar brands Opening of new retail locations will allow Gap to optimize inventory costs in the US, as inventory can be shipped and distributed through already developed channels currently being used by Old Navy, Gap and Banana Republic.

New incentive programs for employees who drive customer feedback surveys will help drive employee loyalty and aid in determining the success of these pilot store locations.

Employee stock options during new initiatives help drive appropriate behavior in employees in all tiers of the organization.

The communication of new store openings and introductions of new team members to lead this initiative will need to be communicated from the Executive Leadership team in order to drive message consistency.

Goal #3: Acquisition of local cotton producers in close proximity where textile producers are located.

Participants: CEO, Head of International Relations, Global Real Estate team and Supply Chain manager.

Steps:

Recently we have seen a rise in cotton prices across the globe. These prices are affecting our textile producers' prices which in turn affect the prices to our customers. We are proposing an option to counter these prices.

We will seek to acquire various cotton farms (1 each year over the next 3 years as pilots) in Delhi, India. These cotton farms are located in close proximity to one of our textile producers Arvind Mills.

By acquiring these farms we will be better able to control our prices through these tough years. If we can acquire multiple farms we will be better equipped to manage situations that would normally cause these farms to raise their prices. If there is a poor yield of crop we will be able to see this problem from the beginning. This would give us a better amount of time to slowly implement a price increase to our customers.

Another advantage to this plan is to have more control over our supplier code of conduct. We will be able to directly oversee how our farms are run. We can implement safety protocols that may not have been abided by previously

This will also allow us to have another control factor into our cost cutting strategy. We will be more able to control our supply prices. Our success has come from squeezing all that we can out of the value chain. These acquisitions will allow us to take our cost cutting to the next level. In the long run we hope to acquire the textile mills as well. At this moment the risk/cost of purchasing these mills in a foreign area highly out ways the advantages. As we expand into these countries and gain better knowledge of their systems this risk reward will start to tip in our favor.

Bibliography

"Company Profile The GAP Inc." *Marketline Report*. EBSCO, 26 Oct. 2012. Web. 6 Nov. 2012. <http://web.ebscohost.com/bsi/pdfviewer/pdfviewer?sid=9337983e-34b3-4dae-8ff5-2b20c1653edc%40sessionmgr114&vid=5&hid=126>.

Gap Inc, Gapinc.com. Site was accessed multiple pages of the website on various dates from September-November 2012.

"GAP Incorporated (The)." *LexisNexis Academic*. W/D Partners, Last revision 22 Nov. 2012. Web. Site was accessed on multiple dates from September – November 2012. <http://www.lexisnexis.com/hottopics/lnacademic/?>.

"GAP Inc, (The)." *LexisNexis Academic Hoovers*. Hoover's Company Records - In-depth Records, Last Revised 27 Nov. 2012. Web. Accessed on various dates from September – November 2012. <http://www.lexisnexis.com/hottopics/lnacademic/>.

"Home." *GAP Inc.com*. GAP Inc, 2012. Web. Site was accessed on multiple dates from September-November 2012. <http://www.gapinc.com/>.

Lovero, Eveann et al. Strategic Management Syllabus. Lewis University. 2011.

Panteva, Nikoleta. "IBISWorld Industry Report 44814." *IBISWorld Where Knowledge Is Power*. N.p., Sept. 2012. Web. 25 Sept. 2012. <http://clients1.ibisworld.com/reports/us/industry/default.aspx?entid=1069>.

"Ross Stores." *LexisNexis Academic*. Worldscope, 26 Nov. 2012. Web. Site was accessed on multiple dates from September – November 2012. <http://www.lexisnexis.com/hottopics/lnacademic/>.

"The Gap, Inc." *EBSCO Host.* DATAMONITOR PLC, 29 Apr. 2011. Web. 16 Sept. 2012.
<http://web.ebscohost.com/bsi/pdfviewer/pdfviewer?vid=22&hid=126&sid=463ae9f6-91ac-
4160-b45c-f186eb380225%40sessionmgr115>.

Thompson, Arthur A., Margart A. Peteraf, John E. Gamble, and A.J. Strickland III. *Crafting and
Executing Strategy: The Quest for Competitive Advantage: Concepts and Cases.* 18th ed. New
York: McGraw-Hill/Irwin, 2012. Print.

"TJX Companies." *LexisNexis Academic.* Worldscope, 26 Nov. 2012. Web. Site was accessed on
multiple dates from September – November 2012.
<http://www.lexisnexis.com/hottopics/lnacademic/>.